THE
DevSecOps
PLAYBOOK

THE
DevSecOps
PLAYBOOK

Deliver Continuous Security at Speed

SEAN D. MACK

Contents at a Glance

CONTENTS

FOREWORD

The friction between traditional security and the rest of the IT organization started increasing as developers needed to deploy more quickly, push out more stable builds, and produce more secure products. Teams created new practices to solve the bottlenecks, and the impossible came into reach. Much like doing multiple deploys a day was once considered insane on the maturity scale, embedding security in the whole organization is now within reach. Security is a first-world citizen in this new alliance between dev and ops.

So how do you get started with DevSecOps? I like people who come to me with solutions instead of complaining about problems. This is how I recruit people with the right attitude. To propose solutions, you need to know what's out there, learn about them, and put them in your toolbox to apply them wisely. Dealing with security is no exception. If you are embarking on this journey, *The DevSecOps Playbook* will provide you with what you need: insights, tools, process, and people practices.

One could say collaboration is all you need, and the rest will come from there. This emphasis on collaboration prompts the question, how is DevSecOps different from DevOps? In mindset there is no difference; they both start from the same principles, similar to how DevOps started from Agile principles. And introducing DevSecOps is no different from driving any other change in a company.

What is important is that by giving DevSecOps its own label, we were able to tag all the related stories and good practices that people were exploring under one umbrella term. The stories and information shared in this book give you the context of how the concept was born. Then you'll learn about the tools and techniques that will help you.

What gives *The DevSecOps Playbook* a unique perspective is that the author has gone through an actual long-running transformation, not just some theoretical exercise. It translates the DevOps principles to security practices. Therefore, instead of focusing on a few aspects, it covers the right broad spectrum of topics. But don't let this vast coverage scare you! It only means that there is a lot to learn. And learn you shall now that you have this book in your hands.

—Patrick Debois

Founder of DevOpsDays and a creator of the DevOps movement

INTRODUCTION

Welcome to *The DevSecOps Playbook: Deliver Continuous Security at Speed*. This book is the definitive guide to DevSecOps transformation. With DevSecOps, you can deliver secure products and services to market quicker, helping you to outpace your competition while ensuring security and privacy. This book explores the people, process, and technology of DevSecOps and provides a guide for driving the transformation.

WHO SHOULD READ THIS BOOK?

This book is intended for anyone interested in truly understanding DevSecOps and how to apply it to keep businesses more secure. More specifically, this book is for security leaders who want to learn about how to drive DevSecOps transformation to build and deliver secure products and services without impeding the flow of delivery. This book is also for security engineers who want a better understanding of DevOps and the changing security landscape, as well as privacy practitioners, auditors, and governance, risk, and compliance specialists who want to understand how a fundamentally different approach to security with DevSecOps can impact the way they do business.

This book is focused on DevSecOps in midsize and large enterprise environments. While the principles of DevSecOps apply to companies of any size, the challenges of coordination and collaboration become more acute with the size and age of a company. Details around driving transformation and organizational structures may be more applicable to companies that have established ways of working than to startups taking a greenfield approach.

A basic understanding of information technology and cybersecurity concepts and terminology may be helpful but is not required.

WHO THIS BOOK IS NOT FOR

This book is not an engineering guide. This book does not tell you how to configure DevSecOps tools (although it covers many tools), and it does not go into detail about secure coding practices.

HOW THIS BOOK IS ORGANIZED

DevSecOps is about more than technology; in fact, it is more about people and collaboration than anything else. Gene Kim, author of the Phoenix Project and one of the foremost thought leaders in DevOps, originally described DevOps as a cultural movement. Because of its cultural nature, DevSecOps impacts all elements of how you do cyber-security. This book uses the classic triad of people, process, and tech-nology to look in depth at all components of DevSecOps.

Chapter 1, "Introducing DevSecOps," starts by providing an overview of DevOps and what DevSecOps is. Chapter 2, "The Evolution of Cybersecurity (from Perimeter to Zero Trust)," provides a foundation for the rest of the book by looking at the evolution of technology and the resulting impact on the approach to cybersecurity. With this background, Chapters 3, "DevSecOps People", Chapter 4, "DevSecOps Process", and Chapter 5, "DevSecOps Technology," look at people, process, and technology and how DevSecOps impacts each of these categories.

The remaining chapters dig into key DevSecOps topics in depth. Chapter 6, "DevSecOps Governance," takes an detailed look at how the concepts of DevSecOps provide a fresh approach to governance and compliance with the opportunity to save millions of dollars and reduce engineering overhead. Chapter 7, "Driving Transformation in Enterprise Environments," provides insight into how to drive the DevSecOps transformation in your business, laying out some of the key elements for successful transformation and some of the pitfalls to avoid. Chapter 8, "Measuring DevSecOps," looks at some of the key metrics for measuring your DevSecOps progress and the impact it is having on the business. Chapter 9, "Conclusion," brings these concepts together by providing some insight into what is coming and the next steps you can take to drive your DevSecOps transformation.

CONVENTIONS USED IN THIS BOOK

Throughout this book you will find a few conventions to note key terms, technical notation, and auxiliary information. The following conventions will help as you make your way through this book:

```
Lines of programming code are noted using this Courier,
fixed-width font.
```

Code that is included within the text looks like these code words within the sentences and paragraphs.

You will also see *key terms* in italics. These are important terms that are given emphasis the first time they appear to indicate their importance.

REAL-WORLD EXAMPLES

Throughout the text, you will find additional information and examples to highlight the points being made through the use of specific, real-world examples.

Key concepts—*Important ideas from the chapter are called out from their context in this manner to make them easily identifiable and to reiterate critical information.*

Notes—*explain background information or clarify a point. They are also used to direct you to information you can find elsewhere to clarify certain topics.*

Tips—*are used throughout the book to provide practical information or advice related to topics covered in the book. These can be helpful in the implementation of the principles covered.*

CHAPTER 1

Introducing DevSecOps

WHY DevSecOps? WHY Now?

DevSecOps provides the ability to deliver more secure products and services to the market rapidly. For decades, technology engineers have sought to balance the speed of delivery with security and performance. DevSecOps fundamentally alters this equation, allowing companies to deliver at speed without compromising security, privacy, or system performance.

Technologists have long struggled with the balance of quality and speed, attempting to answer the question, "How do we deliver products to market quickly without sacrificing security?" With DevSecOps, you finally have that answer, and that answer lies in collaboration. DevOps and, by extension, DevSecOps offer the promised holy grail of technology product development and delivery: the ability to build reliable, secure, and maintainable products without sacrificing speed to market.

DevSecOps provides a fundamentally new approach to security. This approach moves away from the gating approach of yesterday by shifting responsibilities earlier in the development pipeline. By working with developers, it is possible to integrate security across technical applications and services more easily. Through automation and education, one engineer can embed security practices in many applications. By ensuring that security practices are embedded earlier in the developments, you can reduce the effort it takes to build secure products. In effect, by taking a DevOps approach to security, you can reduce the friction of security and compliance and become a force multiplier for the security team.

Cybersecurity has never been a more critical issue than today. The number of cyber threats is continuing to grow. Today we face an increasing number of threats, and the breaches we are seeing have an even larger impact.

With the increasing prevalence of remote work and global teams, the attack surface is continuing to expand. It is no longer possible to simply secure the network perimeter; we must provide security at every level as we move toward approaches such as defense in depth and zero trust. Chapter 2, "The Evolution of Cybersecurity (from Perimeter to Zero Trust)," explores the evolution of the security model in detail.

In addition, we are seeing an increasing number of attackers and increasing sophistication of the attackers. The number of attackers continues to grow as the availability of tools to launch attacks has grown. The ready availability of attack tools means that it takes less skill to launch attacks. Today, a novice attacker can rent a fleet of zombie computers on the Dark Web and launch a distributed denial-of-service attack in minutes. In addition to the proliferation of attackers, we are seeing increasing sophistication of attackers. Today the primary threat actors include organized crime with cybercrime revenue estimated at $1.5 trillion in 2019, more than the revenue of Tesla, Facebook, Microsoft, Apple, Amazon, and Walmart combined.[1] We also see nation-states leveraging cybercrime as a weapon of war.

To combat this increasing threat landscape, you not only need new tools; you need a fundamentally new approach. DevSecOps gives you what you need to combat these emerging threats. By taking a collaborative approach to security, you will be able to leverage the power of the entire technology organization to drive security rather than relying on a single team within that organization. In addition, technologies such as continuous integration and continuous development (CI/CD) allow you to integrate security directly into the deployment pipeline.

---

[1] P., Anton. "Cybercrime Annual Revenue Is 3 Times Bigger than Walmart's." Atlas VPN. AtlasVPN, March 10, 2020. https://atlasvpn.com/blog/cybercrime-annual-revenue-is-3-times-bigger-than-walmarts.

DevOps Overview

The people, process, and technology of DevOps advance the way that engineers build, deploy, and manage technical systems by bridging the gap between development and operations teams to get products to market quickly, while addressing the nonfunctional requirements such as stability and scalability. *DevOps* is a set of principles for delivering value to customers based on Lean principles and collaboration. While many people think of DevOps as a technology or set of technologies, these are really a means to an end. That is, these are simply tools used to better apply the principles of DevOps.[2] DevOps includes the people, processes, and technologies used to deliver value to customers through technical products and services based on the DevOps principles.

DevOps is a set of principles for delivering value to customers based on Lean principles and collaboration.

Gene Kim, DevOps thought leader and author of *The Phoenix Project*: A Novel about IT, DevOps, and Helping Your Business Win\ *The DevOps Handbook:* How to Create World-Class Agility, Reliability, & Security in Technology Organizations, and many other DevOps books, describes DevOps in an interview with Dynatrace, saying, "I think that's exactly what DevOps is. Take those Lean principles, apply them to technology value streams, and you end up with emergent patterns that allow organizations to do tens, hundreds, or even hundreds of thousands of deployments per day, while preserving world-class reliability, security, and stability."

Understanding DevOps as a culture or set of principles that focus on collaboration, you can then understand it as the interaction or collaboration among development, operations, and QA, as shown in Figure 1.1.

---

[2] Virtser, David. "What Is DevOps." Quora. June 22, 2014. www.quora.com/What-is-DevOps/answer/David-Virtser.

Figure 1.1   **DevOps can be thought of as the intersection of development, operations, and quality assurance**

Although there are many definitions of DevOps, the Three Ways of DevOps, described in Gene Kim's *The Phoenix Project*, as well as the CALMS model originated by Jez Humble, co-author of *Accelerate: The Science of Lean Software and DevOps: Building and Scaling High Performing Technology Organizations* and *The DevOps Handbook: How to Create World-Class Agility, Reliability, & Security in Technology Organizations*, provide two of the original models for understanding DevOps. These two models go a long way to explaining the principles underlying DevOps.

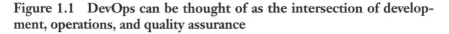

> *If you are already a DevSecOps professional, much of the following information may be review. Feel free to skip to Chapter 2. If you are just getting started with DevOps and DevSecOps, keep reading.*

Brief History of DevOps

In 2009, John Allspaw, then senior vice president of technical operations at Flickr, and Paul Hammond, director of engineering at Flickr, delivered their talk "10+ Deploys per Day: Dev and Ops Cooperation at Flickr" at the O'Reilly Velocity Conference. They introduced many of the concepts of small batch deployment and collaboration between development and operations. The blog *A Short History of DevOps* states that "The talk becomes widely credited with showing the world what development-operations collaboration can achieve."[3] That same year, the term *DevOps* was introduced when Patrick Debois launched the "Devopsdays" event in Ghen, Belgium. The concept took hold, and the first U.S. Devopsdays was held in 2010. Devopsdays was later shortened to the term DevOps that we are all familiar with today.

In 2013, Gene Kim, Kevin Behr, and George Spafford penned their book, *The Phoenix Project: A Novel about IT, DevOps, and Helping Your Business Win*, which presented many of the underpinning concepts that make up DevOps today. At the same time, the "State of DevOps Report" was developed, which sought to determine DevOps best practices and their outcomes. The "State of DevOps Report" has become a staple of information for DevOps practices. In his blog post "A Summary of All of the State of DevOps Reports," Tom Geraghty writes, "The first report was in 2013, and showed quite clearly that adopting DevOps practices resulted in technological and business improvements."

DevOps continued to grow, and in 2014 we saw the increased expansion of DevOps into enterprise environments marked by the launch of the DevOps Enterprise Summit (DOES). DOES sought to explore DevOps at scale for large and complex organizations. That same year the group that would later develp the DevOps Research and Assessment (DORA) metrics teamed up with Puppet labs to find new ways of measuring DevOps and the results.[4] These metrics were included in the "State of DevOps Report" from 2014–2017. The research and details about these metrics were published in *Accelerate: The Science of Lean Software and DevOps: Building and Scaling High Performing Technology Organizations* by Nicole Forsgren, Jez Humble, and Gene Kim in 2018.

While *site reliability engineering* (SRE) had been around for some time, it came into increased usage much later. The term was originally

---

[3] Rapaport, Richard. "A Short History of DevOps." CA Technologies. December 23, 2014. www.ca.com/us/rewrite/articles/devops/a-short-history-of-devops.html.

[4] Humble, Jez. "DORA'S Journey: An Exploration." Medium. February 2, 2019. https://medium.com/@jezhumble/doras-journey-an-exploration-4c6bfc41e667.

used at Google in 2003. The term grew in prominence in the DevOps world around 2015, and in 2017 LinkedIn named SRE as one of the most promising jobs of the year.[5]

It is only in recent years that DevOps has really begun to connect with security and DevSecOps has gained momentum. The 2017 and 2018 "State of DevOps Report" showed that DevOps helped improve security outcomes.

Today, DevOps is something almost every company is doing, from nimble startups to the Fortune 500. More and more the scope is expanding to cover security, and companies are seeing how the benefits of DevOps can be unleashed on cybersecurity through DevSecOps.

The Three Ways of DevOps

Gene Kim's *The Phoenix Project* provides one of the earliest and most widely read explanations of the key principles of DevOps. Based loosely on *The Goal: A Process of Ongoing Improvement* by Eliyahu M. Golratt, *The Phoenix Project* follows a set of fictional characters through the trials of a modern technical and bureaucratic landscape. In the book, the protagonist, Bill Palmer, is thrust into a leadership role as the new VP of operations, where he must right the sinking ship and ensure a successful product launch for a struggling auto parts manufacturer. Through the book he discovers that by getting the development and operations teams to work closely together, he not only saves the struggling project but also boosts the company to never before discovered levels of success.

In the book, Palmer meets a mysterious mentor who guides him through the principles referred to as the *Three Ways of DevOps*. These principles allow Palmer and his team to rise to the challenge.

These "Three Ways" provide some of the core principles of DevOps. On his blog, Kim writes, "We assert that the Three Ways describe the values and philosophies that frame the processes, procedures, practices of DevOps, as well as the prescriptive steps."

Kim describes the Three Ways as follows.

---

[5] Shapero, Daniel. "LinkedIn Data Reveals the Most Promising Jobs of 2017." LinkedIn Official Blog. LinkedIn, January 20, 2017. https://blog.linkedin .com/2017/january/20/linkedin-data-reveals-the-most-promising- jobs-of-2017.

The First Way focuses on the flow through the entire system, which breaks down silos such as development and operations to enable flow from ideation to ultimate customer value creation. This type of thinking shifts focus away from "what is my job?" to "how do we deliver value to the customer?" When viewing systems in this way, people can begin to look at how to maximize flow and remove bottlenecks.

These are examples of the First Way of DevOps:

- **Shared goals**—By sharing goals across technology teams, companies build a shared direction for the company. Instead of having a development team focused on delivering new functionality and an operations team focused on delivering stability, all teams can focus on delivering value to the customer with the right mix of functionality and stability.

- *Value stream mapping*—Value stream analysis is a Lean management technique for analyzing the process of delivering value to the customer. This analysis looks at every step in a process to identify potential bottlenecks and inefficiencies. By mapping out the process of value delivery, it is possible to identify and eliminate bottlenecks that may impact the delivery of value to the customer.

- **Test automation**—Automated development testing is a key element of the First Way, as it reduces handoffs between development and QA teams and eliminates potential bottlenecks, thus enabling the flow of value to the customer. In traditional software development models, software was developed, and once a feature or product was complete, it was handed off to the quality assurance team for testing. Automated testing allows for incremental testing so that minor code changes can be tested as soon as they are checked in. This helps ensure the product is always in a working state during development and eliminates the need for large-scale test and retest cycles at the end of every development cycle.

The Second Way is about creating feedback loops. This way focuses on getting and amplifying input from the customers to the people building the product. The Second Way also includes looking for ways to shorten and amplify these feedback loops.

These are key examples of the Second Way:

- *A/B testing*—A/B testing is the process of comparing and testing hypotheses about a product's performance by testing them in a production environment. As a simple example, if a company wanted to determine if users were more likely to click a green button or a blue button, they could display a green button for 50 percent of users and a blue button for 50 percent of users and measure the results.

- *Feature flags*—Feature flags are a method of turning features on or off. These enable companies to push features to production without making them available to customers and then turn those features on at a given time without additional changes to the code in production. This process allows companies to push new features to production without affecting timing of marketing launches or other timing-related elements. More advance feature flags allow for features to be enabled for certain percentages of users or even certain customer segments and, as such, can enable A/B testing.

- **Continuous customer contact**—One of the best ways to get feedback is by meeting directly with customers. Far too often security engineers work in isolation from the people they are trying to protect. Whether they are internal customers or external customers, it is critical to hear input directly from them at every stage of the product life cycle.

The Third Way focuses on driving experimentation and learning. This includes building a learning culture that is continually reflecting on mistakes, learning from them, and using these learnings to grow and improve. In a learning culture, learning is built into the way a company operates on a daily basis. The Third Way also looks at opportunities to drive mastery through repetition as part of this larger learning culture.

These are key practices of the Third Way:

- *Chaos engineering*—Chaos engineering is a practice where random errors are intentionally inserted into the system to ensure that the system, processes, and people are resilient and able to react and respond appropriately. These errors can range from software defects to hardware failures to security misconfigurations. By inserting errors into the system, chaos engineering helps ensure system resilience and provides opportunities to learn when it is not.

- *20% time*—This refers to the practice of reserving 20 percent of resources time to do work focused on innovation and experimentation. Reserving one day a week or one week a month or 20 percent a day can facilitate this. The key is that this time must be isolated and protected to ensure that there is room for experimentation.

- *Hackathons*—Hackathons are the practice of designating a set period of time where organizations form teams to do focused work on building innovative new ideas. Hackathons often take the form of weeklong efforts focused on demonstration of the work created during that time period.

- *Blameless culture* and *blameless postmortems*—Blameless postmortems focus on providing a safe space to review past incidents without trying to find anyone or any one thing to blame. Instead, these postmortems are focused on using incidents as a learning opportunity, which help the organization improve by learning together. Blameless culture extends this concept ensuring that the culture is one that does not point fingers but instead is one of physiological safety where people can learn and grow.

The Five Ideals

In 2019, Gene Kim released a sequel, *The Unicorn Project: A Novel about Developers, Digital Disruption, and Thriving in the Age of Data*. The Unicorn Project takes place during the same time period at the same company as the Phoenix Project. However, the Unicorn Project follows a second set of characters, giving a perspective from the team level, as they work through their own set of challenges.

Throughout this book, Kim introduces the *Five Ideals*, listed here:

- The First Ideal: Locality and Simplicity
- The Second Ideal: Focus, Flow, and Joy
- The Third Ideal: Improvement of Daily Work
- The Fourth Ideal: Psychological Safety
- The Fifth Ideal: Customer Focus

These ideals introduce ways of working that are crucial to the DevOps culture.

The CALMS Framework

The CALMS framework is another approach to defining the principles of DevOps. CALMS is an acronym that stands for Culture, Automation, Lean, Measurement, and Sharing. The original acronym, CAMS, was coined by John Willis and Damon Edwards. It was later expanded to include *L* for Lean by Jez Humble,[6] co-author of *The DevOps Handbook* and *Continuous Delivery*.

This model focuses on these underlying principles of DevOps:

- Culture focuses on how people work together to achieve a goal.

- Automation emphasizes the need to automate everything through methods like continuous delivery and infrastructure as code to ensure the continuous flow of value to customers. The focus on automation is critical for DevOps because, without it, we require people to take multiple, time-wasting steps, which require handoffs between teams and increase opportunity for bottlenecks.

- Lean refers to the Lean management principles, such as small batch sizes, which underpin much of DevOps. While these principals were originally developed for manufacturing, they

---

[6] Willis, John. "DevOps Culture (Part 1)." IT Revolution. IT Revolution, May 1, 2012. https://itrevolution.com/articles/devops-culture-part-1.

have significant applicability to software engineering. For example, small batch sizes allow for incremental delivery of value to the customer while reducing inventory, backlogs, and work-in-progress.

- Measurement refers to the extraction of key data that provides everyone with constant opportunities to learn and improve.

- Sharing refers to the need for open communication, transparency, and collaboration at all levels and stages of the process.

This model, like the Three Ways, codifies many of the underlying principles of DevOps.

It is important to note that neither the Three Ways nor CALMS excludes security, but neither do they explicitly include security. The focus on removing silos certainly implies that cybersecurity should be part of the value delivery equation.

DevOps as an Anti-Pattern

In many ways, DevOps can be seen as an anti-pattern, a rejection of the idea that operations and development should be separate silos. That is, DevOps has emerged as a response to a common problem that arises in the conflict between operations and development teams.

In traditional software development, with waterfall-based methodology, the development teams and operations teams often function under separate leaders, sometimes even under separate organizations altogether. This organizational structure invites inherent conflict, with development teams focusing on delivering features and operations teams focusing on stability. Not only were these teams focused on separate things, these teams were often aligned around separate and competing goals with compensation tied directly to these goals. Operations teams receive bonuses based on system availability and development teams receive bonuses based on the number of features built. This underlying structure causes conflict between teams and creates delays in getting products to customers, which meet both their functional and nonfunctional requirements.

THE CHANGING RELATIONSHIP BETWEEN DEVELOPMENT AND OPERATIONS

I remember many years ago, applying for my first job leading operations teams. The interviewer asked me how I felt about and handled the conflict between operations and development. Now this was back in the days when the company was still releasing their product on CD, so not only was DevOps not a thing, but many of the enabling technologies hadn't been invented yet.

My answer was something along the lines that it was a healthy tension. This tension was, in fact, useful to have one team that prioritized feature development and another that prioritized stability and, as long as they worked together with open dialogue, a healthy balance would emerge.

My beliefs have changed since then and so has the technology. With the advent of DevOps, we can deliver features to market quickly without sacrificing stability, and these principles apply to security too!

In addition to the inherent conflict based on separation of operations and development teams, this structure coupled with a waterfall-based approach ensured multiple manual handoffs, which, by their nature, create an opportunity for delay.

Development teams handed off the product to the operations teams, who would then begin running through a rigorous set of tests to ensure the application is "ready for production." Only after all development was complete would the operations teams begin looking at the product. Extensive performance testing would be performed, and the maintainability of the product would be reviewed. Invariably, defects were discovered, and the product would be sent back to development for correction. This process fostered a blame-based culture that forced the already burdened development teams to constantly refocus, ensuring further delays.

INHERENT CONFLICT BETWEEN DEVELOPMENT AND OPERATIONS

At another company, I remember sitting cramped in a small conference room with 20 other development and operations engineers fervently arguing with the CTO that the product was not ready to be released. (If you are too young to remember times when this was commonplace, count yourself lucky!) I argued that the product had major known defects and that performance testing was not complete. The CTO was arguing that they had a major market event coming up and the launch of the product was based around this one event. In addition, customers had been promised that this product would be ready, and the date of launch had already been communicated.

I lost that argument. The product was launched with all the known problems. We spent the next two weeks in a struggle to troubleshoot problems while fixing known issues and investigating new complaints. Teams worked day and night just to ensure the product stayed up. The customer experience, and team morale, suffered significantly.

DevOps emerged as a rejection of this approach. With a focus on collaboration, it sought to tear down the barriers between teams, to break through the inherent conflict between development and operations, and, in so doing, to deliver better products to market that addressed both the functional and nonfunctional requirements in a much timelier and more transparent way.

Agile and DevOps

Both the Agile and DevOps methodologies have roots in Lean manufacturing. Dating back to the 1990s, Agile focuses on development and quality assurance working together to deliver incremental value to customers. While more recent, DevOps takes these same concepts and extends them to operations, building on many of the same principles and practices.

If you look at the goals of Agile and DevOps, you find that they are strikingly similar. Look at the value Agile and DevOps deliver. That is, look at the "why" of DevOps, and look at the "why" of Agile. When you look closer, you discover that the goals of both are to get value to the customer quicker and to rapidly react to changing market demands. DevOps takes the principles introduced in Agile and extends them beyond code check-in to deployment and operations.

DevOps takes the principles introduced in Agile and extends them beyond code check-in to deployment and operations.

As the goals of Agile and DevOps align, it is not surprising to find significant overlap in the practices that surround them. In many ways, the intersection of DevOps and Agile relates to a culture of collaboration and modern technical practices and processes that emerge from that culture. Processes such as continuous testing and the small batch deployment help ensure the rapid delivery of working products to the customer. DevOps takes Agile concepts and extends them beyond the build so you can amplify Agile by implementing DevOps practices.[7]

DevOps and ITSM

There is a prevalent myth that DevOps and IT Service Management (ITSM) and the IT Infrastructure Library (ITIL) are incompatible. However, this supposition has very little basis. ITIL is a framework from which you can take or leave portions you like, and, in fact, this framework provides many useful paradigms for DevOps implementations.

Contrary to the myth, there is a considerable amount of synergy between ITIL and DevOps. If you understand ITIL as a process framework and see DevOps as, primarily, a culture of collaboration, there is no reason you cannot have a process framework integrate very well with a culture of collaboration. In fact, the process framework of ITIL can support the culture of collaboration. If you look at the ITIL

---

[7] Mack, Sean. "Innovate ITIL: A DevOps Approach to the ITIL Framework." DZone. August 2, 2018. https://dzone.com/articles/innovate-itil-a-devops-approach-to-the-itil-framew.

process for problem management, incident management, or change management and approach these with a focus on DevOps principles such as collaboration, transparency, learning, and automation, you can build DevOps-aligned processes to support the business.

Many others have noted the synergies between DevOps and ITIL. At CIO.com, Barclay Rae writes, "We need the key elements that are found in both ITSM and DevOps, whether we use these explicitly or not. DevOps is much more than just automated development; it involves collaboration and a blame-free culture. As well, ITSM/ITIL shouldn't be pigeonholed as an administrative burden, but rather used in an Agile way."[8]

The ITIL process framework is just that, a framework. It is not a mandate that "thou must fill out 20 pages of documents to release software" (although some overly bureaucratic implementations certainly make it feel that way). When you understand the IT Infrastructure Library as a framework, it becomes evident that there is no reason you cannot apply DevOps principles within this framework to make your technology operations more streamlined. By taking a DevOps approach to your change process definition and implementation, you can drive safer releases rapidly, you can ensure better communication between your teams, you can drive quicker resolution to incidents, and you can ensure you keep your focus keenly on delivering value to your customers quickly.[9] You will delve deeper into how you can take a DevOps approach to ITIL processes in Chapter 4, "DevSecOps Process."

DevSecOps Overview

Put simply, DevSecOps is the subset of DevOps focused on cybersecurity. It is critical to fully understand DevOps. In many ways, DevSecOps is the intersection of development, quality assurance, operations, and cybersecurity, as shown in Figure 1.2.

---

[8] Rae, Barclay. "ITSM Vs. DevOps: Which Side Are You On?" CIO. May 15, 2017. www.cio.com/article/229983/itsm-vs-devops-which-side-are-you-on.html.
[9] Mack, Sean, and Christopher Lee. "Amplify Agile With DevOps." LinkedIn. May 19, 2020. www.linkedin.com/pulse/amplify-agile-devops-sean-d-mack-mba.

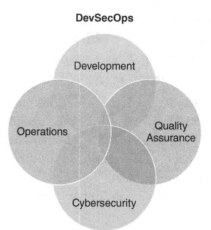

Figure 1.2 DevSecOps can be though of as intersection of development, operations, quality assurance, and cybersecurity.

Agile focuses on the overlap of development and quality assurance; DevOps focuses on the interconnectivity between development, quality assurance, and operations; and DevSecOps focuses on the connection between development, quality assurance, operations, and cybersecurity (see Figure 1.3).

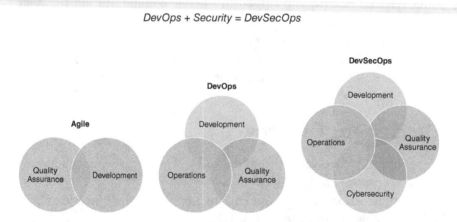

Figure 1.3 While Agile focuses on the development process, DevOps adds focus on the operational aspects of the product life cycle, and DevSecOps emphasizes security.

This view of Agile, DevOps, and DevSecOps is, perhaps, a bit too simplistic. Agile never excluded operations or security. In fact, it provides a model for prioritizing operations and security work. In addition, the small batch sizes and rapid iteration are ideally suited for reducing the scope of defects that might be introduced and addressing them rapidly when they are introduced.

Similarly, DevOps never explicitly excluded cybersecurity. In fact, DevOps was always meant to include it. As DevOps is based on the idea that value can be delivered faster through collaboration, we should expect that this collaboration should extend to security. In the article "Surprise! Broad Agreement on the Definition of DevOps," Eric Minick writes of "community leaders and analysts writing, 'No, no it really should be Dev____Ops' where the blank is filled in by their own specialty. Examples are DevQAOps, DevOpsSec, DevSecOps, BizDevOps, and, of course, Bussdevtestqanetsecnetops."[10] But, of course, Bussdevtestqanetsecnetops would not have caught on as well as DevOps. The point is that DevOps is meant to be inclusive and, as such, should certainly include cybersecurity.

But too often it does not. Security teams are frequently excluded from the DevOps discussion. It is also the case that security teams have been slow to adapt to the DevOps mindset. With a culture rooted in risk mitigation, security teams are often accustomed to operating in a silo surrounded by secrecy. By their nature, the data that security teams deal with can be highly sensitive and require higher levels of secrecy. This confidential nature and secretive culture has, in many cases, delayed adoption of DevOps principles around transparency and collaboration. It is the purpose of this book to explore how the DevOps principles can be applied to cybersecurity in a way that does not compromise the privacy or security of the customer data. While it is possible to break down the walls between teams and make security an integral part of product development, it requires a shift of technical practices and cultural norms.

RUGGED DevOps OVERVIEW

Like DevSecOps, Rugged DevOps is an extension of DevOps that places a priority on security. Rugged DevOps is based on the *Rugged Software movement*, which was started by Joshua Corman, David Rice,

---

[10] Minick, Eric. "Surprise! Broad Agreement on the Definition of DevOps." DevOps. Com. May 13, 2015. https://devops.com/surprise-broad-agreement-on-the-definition-of-devops.

and Jeff Williams in 2010. The Rugged Software movement focuses on developing software that was highly available, secure, and resilient. Similar to DevOps, Rugged Software also emphasizes the cultural aspects of software development focusing on organizational elements such as cooperation and experimentation.[11]

In 2012, Corman, Rice, and Williams teamed up with several others to publish the Rugged Handbook, which included the Rugged Manifesto. The Rugged Manifesto laid out the core principles of Rugged Software development as follows:

> I am rugged because I refuse to be a source of vulnerability or weakness.
>
> I am rugged because I assure my code will support its mission.
>
> I am rugged because my code can face these challenges and persist in spite of them.
>
> I am rugged, not because it is easy, but because it is necessary and I am up for the challenge.

Rugged DevOps is similar to DevSecOps in that both are based on DevOps and focus on security. However, where Rugged focuses on prioritizing security, DevSecOps focuses on collaboration and extending the principles of DevOps to security.

DevSecOps BUSINESS RESULTS

It is important when you approach any sort of transformation that you look at the "why." You must truly understand the motivating factors that justify a costly and time-consuming undertaking. It is not enough to do DevOps simply because it is the latest buzzword or because your

---

[11] Corman, Joshua, David Rice, and Jeff Williams. "The Rugged Manifesto." Rugged Software. February 5, 2010. https://ruggedsoftware.org.

boss told you to do it. If you are undertaking an effort that will require a substantial amount of work and fundamentally shift the culture of your company, you must do it to achieve bottom-line business results.

The 2021 "State of DevOps Report" by the DevOps Research and Assessment (DORA) team at Google Cloud provided details about the impact that DevOps is having for high-performing organizations. The report found that high-performing DevOps teams deploy code 973 times more frequently than low performers. These teams also had a lead time to change (as measured by the time from code commit to code deploy) 6,570 times faster than the lower-performing teams.

In addition, these same high-performing teams had a mean failure rate less than a third (7.5 percent versus 23 percent) of their lower-performing counterparts. And, when failures did occur, they restored service 6,570 times faster than low-performing teams.[12] So, not only are high-performing teams delivering code faster to production, but they are also providing far greater levels of availability.

BUSINESS RESULTS FROM DevOps

We saw this same sort of business-level improvement in our implementation of DevOps at Wiley & Sons Ltd. During the rollout of DevOps, the average flow time, as measured from code commit to production, dropped by 11 percent. In addition, the lead time, as measured by flow time plus time in the backlog, decreased by 9 percent.

(continues)

---

[12] Kersten, Nigel, McCarthy, Kate, & Stahnke, Michael. 2021 State of DevOps Report. Puppet, 2021.

(continued)

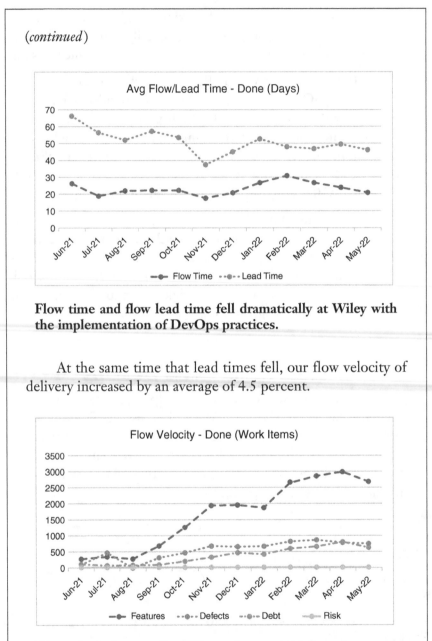

Flow time and flow lead time fell dramatically at Wiley with the implementation of DevOps practices.

At the same time that lead times fell, our flow velocity of delivery increased by an average of 4.5 percent.

Flow velocity increased at Wiley as the pace of delivery improved.

Not only were we able to deliver software to market faster, but we saw significant improvements in stability. Our average

(continued)

mean time to restore (MTTR) improved by 25 percent, with MTTR for top-priority incidents (P1) improving by 83 percent!

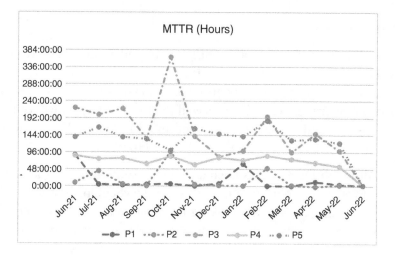

The time to resolve issues as measured by MTTR fell across all incident priorities.

Perhaps most important, overall employee engagement increased by 2 percent while these massive changes and improvements were happening.

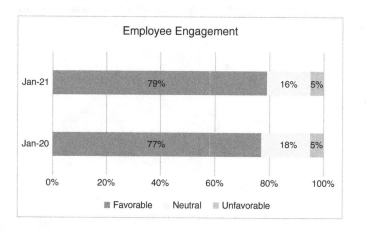

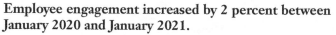

Employee engagement increased by 2 percent between January 2020 and January 2021.

If you can see these sorts of changes by implementing DevOps, think about the benefits when you begin to use these same principles for cybersecurity.

CONCLUSION

DevSecOps takes the principles of DevOps and applies them to security. Drawing from Lean and focusing on collaboration, DevSecOps presents a fundamentally new approach to cybersecurity. DevSecOps draws on the principles of Lean as well as others, such as flow, continuous learning, and automation codified in Kim's Three Ways and the CALMS model from Willis, Edwards, and Humble.

Although DevOps has been around for some time now and is, in many ways, entering a more mature state, DevSecOps is still new for many companies. If you are looking for a better way to do cybersecurity and if you are interested in learning how to take what people have learned from DevOps and apply those principles to security, keep reading.

The following chapters explore how the principles of DevOps can be applied to all aspects of cybersecurity. From people to process to technology, DevSecOps requires a different approach, but this new approach delivers real results. Taking a collaborative approach to cybersecurity and applying the principles of DevOps will enable you to deliver software faster without sacrificing security.

CHAPTER 2

The Evolution of Cybersecurity (from Perimeter to Zero Trust)

THE EVOLUTION OF THE THREAT LANDSCAPE

To best understand DevSecOps, it should be understood in the broader context of the evolution of technology and cybersecurity. DevSecOps has emerged, in part, because technologies such as CI/CD enable companies to work in new ways.

Evolution of Infrastructure

Since the 1980s, massive shifts in the technology landscape have given rise to new threats and new security responses. One of the most fundamental to the cybersecurity approach is the expansion and erosion of the network perimeter. DevSecOps offers key strategies for addressing these new challenges.

Traditional cybersecurity approaches focused on securing the perimeter. This made sense in legacy network environments where all of the critical systems and data for a company were contained within the company walls. When all the company's data, systems, and employees were located in one location, securing that location was enough. By providing network security at the perimeter, engineers could provide a walled garden, thus protecting the crown jewels within. However, as technology has moved from a centrally hosted, on-premises model to a cloud-based model, the validity of this approach has rapidly deteriorated. The "Verizon 2022 Data Breach Investigation Report" notes that "the main ways in which your business is exposed to the Internet are the main ways that your business is exposed to the bad guys."[1] As this perimeter has become increasingly complex and porous, new approaches to cybersecurity have had to emerge.

The proliferation of the Internet has been a major factor in expanding the ways in which attackers can gain access to corporate resources. Since the launch of the public Internet in 1991, the borders for business have been continuing to expand. If you look back on the history of cyber-attacks, it highlights this point. The AIDS Trojan, also known as PC Cyborg Trojan, was the first example of *ransomware*, a class of breach used to extort money from a company. This Trojan horse was distributed in 1989 via thousands of floppy disks, which were mailed to users and installed when unsuspecting users ran the program on the disk. This is a stark reminder that, at that time, to access users' systems, one had to be physically near a system or introduce malicious code. Today, with the ubiquity of email and the Internet, all attackers need to do is get users to click a link to download malicious code.

This same issue has been significantly worsened as companies have increasingly moved to globally distributed, hybrid (work-from-home/corporate office) workforces and work-from-anywhere models. When all people working at a company were physically located at a company's office, providing strong premise-based network perimeter security was an effective security mechanism. However, with the advent of COVID-19, more companies are implementing hybrid workforce strategies with a significantly larger percentage of the population working from home. According to Gallup research, as of October 2021, 45 percent of full-time employees work from home at least part of the time.[2] This means that the attack surface that attackers can focus on is no longer limited to the periphery of the network and the office—now the attack surface extends to employees homes, to airports, and to public parks, in fact, today's workforce may be anywhere there is a network connection.

---

[1] Bassett, Gabriel, C. D. Hylender, Phillip Langlois, Alex Pinto, and Suzanne Widup. 2022. Data Breach Investigations Report. Verizon.
[2] Saad, Lydia, and Ben Wigert. "Remote Work Persisting and Trending Permanent." Gallup. October 13, 2021. https://news.gallup.com/poll/355907/remote-work-persisting-trending-permanent.aspx.

In addition, companies are increasingly moving to bring-your-own-device (BYOD) policies, which allow unsecured and unmanaged devices onto the corporate network. In the *Forbes* article "BYOD Reignited: How to Get It Right This Time," Dean Hager notes that, after a downturn in 2018, the COVID-19 pandemic has reignited the move for employees to bring their own devices to work. Figures 2.1.1–2.1.7 illustrates the continued expansion and growing complexity of the threat surface landscape.

Figure 2.1.1   Early computer systems and data were contained in the company headquarters or the mainframes which were often located within the headquarters.

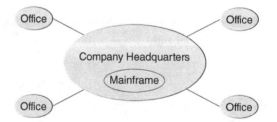

Figure 2.1.2   Interconnected offices expanded the network footprint.

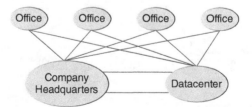

Figure 2.1.3   Data centers were co-located or hosted outside of the company headquarters further expanding the network perimeter and data footprint.

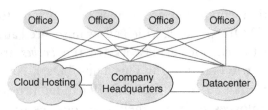

Figure 2.1.4 Increased adoption of cloud providers such as AWS, GCP, and Azure provided new locations for companies' data, applications, and services.

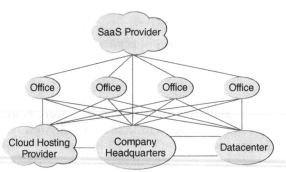

Figure 2.1.5 SaaS providers such as Salesforce and SAP introduced new locations where critical data resides outside the direct control of the company.

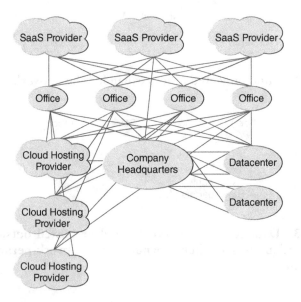

Figure 2.1.6 As cloud adoption accelerated multi-cloud approach further increased the spread of company data.

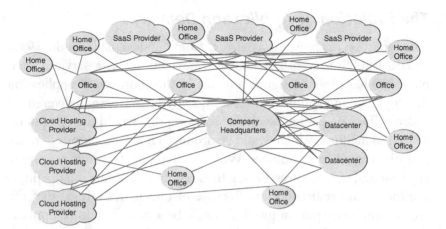

Figure 2.1.7   The global remote and hybrid work environment acceler-ated by the COVID-19 pandemic rapidly increased the locations where employees are working adding further complexity to companies' network.

Having a "a hard crunchy outside and a soft chewy center" is no longer a viable security posture.[3]

Because of the increasingly complex perimeter, cybersecurity must move away from simply securing the perimeter, an approach often referred to as the *castle-and-moat* approach. Simply having a cas-tle and moat is no longer sufficient, nor is it practical if the land you are trying to protect extends well beyond the castle walls. Today, you must assume that you need to protect people and land well beyond the cas-tle. You must also assume the enemy is already inside. As Stephanie Balaouras noted in her 2010 Forrester report, having a "a hard crunchy outside and a soft chewy center" is no longer a viable security posture. Today's security approach must provide security at every layer, from the network to the application to the database. This has given rise to the concepts of *Defense in Depth* and Zero Trust security, which are explored later in this chapter.

---

[3] Kindervag, John. 2010. No More Chewy Centers: Introducing The Zero Trust Model Of Information Security. Forrester.

The Evolution of Application Delivery

The evolution of application delivery from physical media in the 1990s and early 2000s to web-based updates and software-as-a-service (SaaS) platforms has played a significant role in the approach to application development and application security. Early software was delivered via disk or CD. Companies developed software that would then be put on a physical medium, which would be produced many thousands of times and distributed to customers. With this type of distribution system, any changes, new features, or bug fixes required reproducing the physical media and redistribution. Because of this, it was critical that the application being put on physical media be a fully functional application with as few defects as possible.

Developing a fully functional, complete product and distributing it via physical media made the idea of incremental updates or small batch delivery impractical, if not impossible. Software updates required physical shipment of thousands of new disks or CDs. This is analogous to automotive production. A car is developed and delivered with all the features that it will have for the life cycle of the vehicle. Only in extreme circumstances such as major defects are cars updated during their life cycle. In these cases, a recall is issued, and manufacturers must spend millions, and in some cases billions, of dollars.

Development methodologies such as waterfall were developed for the type of applications that were being built and the distribution mechanism of the time. With the ubiquity of the Internet and the ability to not only deliver software over the Internet, but also to update that software regularly over the Internet, delivering in small batch updates became a reality. This same principle is extended with SaaS applications. SaaS applications—such as Salesforce, Microsoft 365, and Slack—are hosted and managed by the provider and do not require delivery or installation. SaaS-based applications can be instantly updated by the software vendor for all users by updating the hosted platform.

It is important to keep in mind that legacy software development methodologies were not "wrong" but that new technologies have emerged that enable DevOps and DevSecOps. With an understanding of the technologies behind this shift, you may be better able to leverage it correctly and be prepared for the next shift.

The Evolution of the Threat Landscape

Since the 1970s, cybercriminals have been finding new ways to attack systems. As the attack surface has increased and the value of breaches has increased, so too has the ferocity of the attacks. Attacks have evolved from relatively simple worms written by individual developers to advanced, multistage attacks launched by nation-states.

Computer viruses date as far back as the 1970s. One of the first ever computer viruses was written by Bob Thomas in 1971 as a simple computer program designed to move between computers on ARPANET, the predecessor to the Internet.[4] The program simply moved between computers and displayed the message "I'm the Creeper: catch me if you can!" and was subsequently named the Creeper. Bob Thomas's colleague Ray Tomlinson responded by writing a program that similarly moved between computers and deleted the Creeper, which became known as the "the Reaper," thus the Reaper and the Creeper. While the Creeper did not have malicious intent or create significant damage, it was a portent of things to come and the ongoing battle between hackers and defenders. It was also evidence of the power and the danger of computers that were connected, a danger that grew exponentially with the launch of the Internet.

In 1988, the first *Denial-of-Service* attack was launched. Denial-of-Service attacks attempt to render resources unavailable by making a large number of requests with the intention of overloading the resource such as application servers. The first such instance was an Internet worm, dubbed the "Morris worm" after its creator, Robert Tappan Morris, a student at Cornell University. The source code is as follows:

```
static mainloop()                        /* 0x2302 */
{
    long key, time1, time0;
    time(&key);
    srandom(key);
    time0 = key;
    if (hg() == 0 && hl() == 0)
     ha();
```

---

[4] Wikipedia contributors, "Creeper and Reaper," Wikipedia, The Free Encyclopedia, https://en.wikipedia.org/w/index.php?title=Creeper _and_Reaper&oldid=1155116768.

```
checkother();
report_breakin();
cracksome();
other_sleep(30);

while (1) {
    /* Crack some passwords */
  cracksome();
  /* Change my process id */
  if (fork() > 0)
      exit(0);

  if (hg() == 0 && hi() == 0 && ha() == 0)
      hl();
  other_sleep(120);
  time(&time1);
  if (time1 - time0 >= 60*60*12)
      h_clean();
  if (pleasequit && nextw > 0)

      exit(0);
}
```

}[5]

While its creator claimed it was intended simply to gauge the size of the Internet, a bug in the code led it to infect the same computer multiple times causing it to crash.[6] Morris was subsequently convicted of a felony under the Computer Fraud and Abuse Act.[7] Critically, the Morris worm prompted the creation of the Computer Emergency Response Team (CERT), a federally funded research center focused on improving the security of software and the Internet.

[5] Martini, Arialdo. "Arialdomartini / Morris-worm." GitHub. November 24, 2020. https://github.com/arialdomartini/morris-worm/blob/master/worm.c.
[6] "The Fascinating Evolution of Cybersecurity." La Trobe University. February 15, 2018. www.latrobe.edu.au/nest/fascinating-evolution-cybersecurity.
[7] Wikipedia contributors, "Morris worm," Wikipedia, The Free Encyclopedia, https://en.wikipedia.org/w/index.php?title=Morris_worm&oldid=1161946775.

The 1990s saw the proliferation of email-based attacks against enterprises—such as "Melissa" and "ILOVEYOU"—which led to the rise in antivirus software and gave birth to the companies that would dominate cybersecurity protection for years to come. During this time, the proliferation of the Internet also gave rise to many more paths to launch an attack, otherwise known as *attack vectors*. Self-replicating popup ads were at first just a nuisance but increasingly gave rise to more invasive malware, spyware, and trojans.

The 2000s saw the evolution toward attacks on corporations to steal consumer information with large-scale data breaches, like the 2007 data breach of TJ Maxx. It was, at the time, the largest breach of consumer data, with up to 45.6 million stolen credit and debit card numbers.

Since the 2010s, attacks have evolved to be increasingly complex and breadth. The 2014 attack on Target's retail point of sale compromised more than 40 million credit and debit card accounts. In 2017, the Equifax data breach exposed the private data of more than 150 million people.

More recently, the rise of well-funded, organized crime syndicates and nation-state actors driving major cybercrime attacks has exposed existential and global vulnerabilities. These attacks are increasingly sophisticated, with multiple attack vectors. In addition, attacks include complex movement from the breached system to adjacent systems, commonly referred to as *lateral movement*, once breaches have occurred. This has corresponded with a rise in ransomware attacks precipitated by the emergence of crypto currencies, making it easier to collect payment and more difficult to track the source of the attacker.

In conjunction, there has been an increase in *supply chain attacks*, attacks aimed at intermediaries to get to the intended targets. Supply chain attacks include attacks on intermediary vendors, open-source products, or products and services that are used as part of the software development process. The SolarWinds breach in 2020 was one of the best-known examples of a supply chain attack, where attackers injected malicious code into Orion, the enterprise network monitoring tool used by more than 18,000 customers.

Cybersecurity continues to evolve with attacks growing in frequency and scale. Cybersecurity professionals must proactively and rapidly evolve their approach if they are to keep their customers and companies safe.

THE EVOLUTION OF CYBERSECURITY RESPONSE

As the threat landscape has developed, so too has the responses to these threats. To address the growing complexity of the attack surface and the veracity of the attackers, new methods of defense have had to evolve. Both Defense in Depth and Zero Trust have emerged as ways to address this changing landscape. The concepts included in these approaches underpin many of the approaches taken in DevSecOps.

Defense in Depth

Defense in Depth takes a layered approach to security, providing security at every layer of operations and infrastructure. The National Institute of Standards and Technology (NIST) defines *Defense in Depth* as "Information security strategy integrating people, technology, and operations capabilities to establish variable barriers across multiple layers and dimensions of the organization."[8]

Defense in Depth came from the National Security Agency (NSA) and was developed based on a military strategy with the same name. "The Defense in Depth (DiD) originated in the military arena as a defensive strategy aimed to protect the population while preserving the effectiveness of defense installations. It deals with slowdown of the progression of an attack by using different successive layers, such as fortifications, troops, and field works, instead of concentrating all resources onto a single defensive line."[9]

Defense in Depth recognizes that, because the perimeter is deteriorating and/or even nonexistent, it is necessary to have defense at every layer. If a perimeter exists at all, you must assume the attacker has

---

[8] "Defense-in-depth." NIST Computer Security Resource Center CSRC. NIST, February 15, 2018. https://csrc.nist.gov/glossary/term/defense_in_depth.

[9] Chierici, Lorenzo, Gian Luigi Fiorini, Stefano La Rovere, and Paolo Vestrucci3. "The Evolution of Defense in Depth Approach: A Cross Sectorial Analysis." Open Journal of Safety Science and Technology Vol. 6, no. No. 2 (2016). Accessed March 31, 2022. https://doi.org/10.4236/ojsst.2016.62004.

already breached it and ensure that other attack vectors are protected as well. In addition, Defense in Depth recognizes that security is not limited to the perimeter but rather extends beyond technology to the people involved.

As illustrated in Figure 2.2, this layering approach should include the following:

- Perimeter
- Network
- Host
- Application
- Data

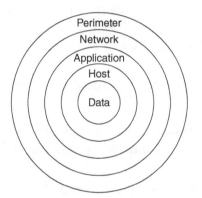

Figure 2.2   Defense in Depth takes a layered approach to security with protection at every level.

At each layer, different security measures are put in place to protect that layer. Protections at each layer include items such as these:

- *Perimeter security* includes the physical and technical boundaries, including things such as physical security (e.g., deadbolt locks), intrusion detection systems (IDSs), and email security.

- *Network security* includes all security related to the networks that an organization uses to transmit information and may include items such as firewalls, demilitarized zones (DMZs), and virtual private networks (VPNs).

- *Application security* includes all security of the technical applications and services and includes vulnerability scanners, software composition analysis (SCA), static application security testing (SAST), and dynamic application security testing (DAST).

- *Data security* includes the protection of a company's digital information. Protection at this layer includes things such as identity and access management (IAM), data classification, and encryption.

While this list is in no way meant to be comprehensive, it should clearly illustrate that, even within a layer, several types of protection may be required. Robyn Wright, CISO at Wiley, uses the analogy of a house that needs protecting. You may need a fence and a camera to protect the area around your house as well as window locks and door locks to ensure no one enters. The door itself may even have multiple types of locks. When you look at protecting the enterprise business, many options may be needed at each layer—the number and types of those protections will depend on the size, maturity, and risk tolerance of a given organization.

In addition to providing technology solutions at each layer of the system, Defense in Depth includes operational and governance activities by both people and technology. These leverage the tooling at each layer to help ensure the security of the system as a whole. *Telemetry* is the measurement data collected by the tools and instrumentation designed to measure a systems performance. Operations teams leverage telemetry within the systems to provide 24/7/365 support and response when critical issues arise.

Governance functions track the data to ensure that not only are companies adhering to compliance requirements but also that the tools are operating effectively. For example, a governance team may be responsible for tracking all vulnerabilities reported from various sources and ensuring that they are remediated within specified *service level agreements (SLAs)*. It should be noted that, when taking a DevSecOps approach, it is critical that operations and governance functions work in tight collaboration with application development teams and not as separate silos (see Figure 2.3). Chapter 7, "Driving Transformation in Enterprise Environments," covers this in more detail. For now, suffice to say that having a governance body that functions as a separate silo to impose rules on development teams is antithetical to the DevSecOps approach.

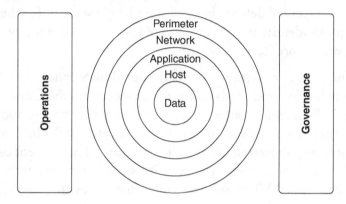

Figure 2.3   In addition to security at every level, Defense in Depth includes operational and governance activities to help manage across all the layers.

With the disintegration of the perimeter, network or perimeter security is no longer enough. The modern enterprise requires a Defense in Depth that includes defense at each layer as well as governance and operational management to coordinate across all layers.

Zero Trust

Like Defense in Depth, *Zero Trust* is another strategy to address the perimeterless business world we operate in today. Zero Trust provides a new approach to security that is based around the idea that organizations should never automatically assume trusted relationships and should always require verification. The key concept of Zero Trust strategy is "never trust, always verify." NIST Special Publication 800-207 defines Zero Trust as "a security concept centered on the belief that organizations should not automatically trust anything inside or outside its perimeters and instead must verify anything and everything trying to connect to its systems before granting access."[10]

Zero Trust may rely on Defense in Depth strategies, but the two are not the same. While Defense in Depth focuses on providing security at every layer, Zero Trust focuses on the assumption that trust should never be assumed. So, it is quite possible that a company could have many layers of defense but still use a single source of authentication to prove identity that's then accepted at every layer and, therefore, not adhere to core Zero Trust principles.

The term *Zero Trust* was initially coined by Stephen Paul Marsh in 1994 in his doctoral thesis on computer security at the University of Stirling in Scotland. In attempting to quantify the trust relationship, Marsh describes situations in which trust equaled 0.[11] However, the NIST special publication on Zero Trust notes, "The concept of Zero Trust has been present in cybersecurity since before the term 'Zero Trust' was coined." The special publication notes that work in the Jericho Forum in 2004 as well as work by the Defense Information Systems Agency (DISA) and the Department of Defense discussing security approaches moving away from perimeter-based security.

In 2009, the concept took a significant step forward when Google implemented a Zero Trust architecture referred to as BeyondCorp. BeyondCorp is a cybersecurity architecture that developed access policies based on a specific device, the device state, and the user. The term was popularized in 2010 by John Kindervag, an analyst at Forester Research in his publication "No More Chewy Centers: Introducing The Zero Trust Model Of Information Security."[12] This concept was

---

[10] Rose, Scott, Oliver Borchert, Stu Mitchell, and Sean Connelly. "Zero Trust Architecture." (2020). Accessed March 31, 2022. https://doi.org/10.6028/NIST.SP.800-207.

[11] Marsh, Stephen P. "Formalising Trust as a Computational Concept." Submitted in partial fulfilment of the degree of Doctor of Philosophy, University of Stirling, 1994.

[12] Kindervag, John. "No More Chewy Centers: The Zero Trust Model Of Information Security." Forrester, (2016). Accessed March 31, 2022.

expanded on in 2018 when NIST published Special Publication 800-207, "Zero Trust Architecture," and in 2021 when the *Cybersecurity and Infrastructure Security Agency (CISA)*, an agency of the United States Department of Homeland Security, published version 1.0 of the Zero Trust Maturity Model, which defined the five pillars of Zero Trust.[13]

The Cybersecurity & Infrastructure Security Agency defines the five pillars of Zero Trust as follows:

- **Identity**—Attributes that allow systems to uniquely recognize an entity that is trying to take action. Zero Trust has several approaches to identity including least privilege access, movement away from password toward combination of factors, and the need to continuously validate access, not just when originally granted.

- **Device**—Any hardware asset that can connect to a network. The Zero Trust Maturity Model entails not just validating the identity of users but also ensuring the security of each device they use to access services and data.

- **Network/environment**—The medium over which digital communications flow, whether that be wireless, local area networks, or the Internet. Zero Trust identifies various methods for secure network design, including *segmentation*, the process of dividing the network into multiple discrete sections, and *micro-segmentation*, which breaks the network down into even smaller segments based on individual workloads. Network protections also include encryption and machine-learning based threat protection.

- **Application workload**—Applications and services managed by the company corresponding to the application layer in the Defense-in-Depth approach. Recommended activities for protecting application workloads can include continuous authorization, behavioral analysis, and integrated security testing as part of the deployment pipeline.

---

[13] "Zero Trust Maturity Model." Cybersecurity and Infrastructure Security Agency Cybersecurity Division 1.0, (2021). Accessed March 31, 2022.

- **Data**—The company's data assets at rest and in transit, whether it be on devices, inside storage devices, or part of databases. Zero Trust protection techniques for data include tagging and categorization for tracking purposes, encryption, and strict access-based controls.

For additional information about Zero Trust and the implementation methods for the five pillars of Zero Trust, see the 2021 CISA publication "Zero Trust Maturity Model."

It is important to note that both Defense in Depth and Zero Trust have often been coopted as buzzwords by marketing teams. While both provide valuable security models, they are often used to sell products in misleading ways. Because of this, products are often sold as "Zero Trust Solutions." This has added confusion to the definition of these terms, as companies have used them to fit their products rather than as originally intended. Defense in Depth and Zero Trust are security concepts that must be applied wholistically and cannot be solved by any one product or service.

Shift Left

Shift Left is the concept of doing tasks earlier in the development process than they are traditionally done. While Shift Left originally focused on moving testing earlier in the development process, the concept, and the related benefits, can be extended to reliability engineering and security engineering practices. By testing earlier in the development process, you can significantly reduce the time and effort it takes to address these issues—these same benefits can be enjoyed when applied to security. Shift Left has become a critical component of DevOps and DevSecOps because of the applicability to small batch delivery/CI/CD and alignment with DevOps principles.

In traditional waterfall development methodologies, the software development process is displayed left to right, from plan to develop to test to deploy (see Figure 2.4). In this model, systems were fully built and integrated with other systems before testing begins in earnest.

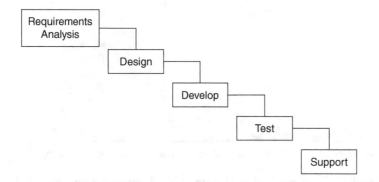

Figure 2.4 Traditional waterfall development methodology depicted as proceeding from left to right from requirements analysis to support.

The Shift Left testing approach takes advantage of the fact that, by doing testing earlier in the development process, the cost of identifying and remediating defects is significantly reduced.

The term was originally introduced by Larry Smith, the chief scientist emeritus of software productivity research (SPR), in his article, "Shift-Left Testing" in September 2001. In this article, Smith writes, "Shift-left testing is how I refer to a better way of integrating the quality assurance (QA) and development parts of a software project. By linking these two functions at lower levels of management, you can expand your testing program while reducing manpower and equipment needs—sometimes by as much as an order of magnitude."[14]

While waterfall models generally include some test work up front, such as development of test plans, the vast majority of it is done at the end of the test cycle, leaving many defects to be found very far into a project (see Figure 2.5).

The Shift Left model of testing brings much of the testing up front, as shown in Figure 2.6.

---

[14] Smith, Larry. "Shift-Left Testing." Dr. Dobb's Journal, (2001). Accessed May 31, 222. https://web.archive.org/web/20140810171940/http://collaboration.cmc.ec.gc.ca/science/rpn/biblio/ddj/Website/articles/DDJ/2001/0109/0109e/0109e.htm.

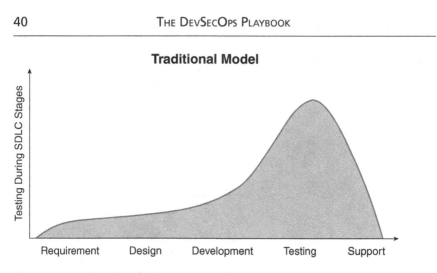

Figure 2.5 Testing during the traditional development cycle is heavily weighted toward the end of the cycle.

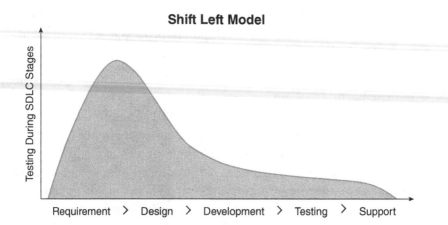

Figure 2.6 Testing by development phase using a Shift Left approach introduces significantly higher levels of testing at the beginning of the development cycle.

The practice of shifting left exemplifies Gene Kim's First and Second Ways of DevOps. By shifting testing earlier in the process, you reduce the time to identify and remediate issues, thus increasing flow of value key to Kim's First Way of DevOps. In addition, shifting testing left helps amplify and shorten feedback loops, illustrating the Second Way of DevOps. By doing security testing closer to when the code is actually being produced, you shorten the amount of time between development and feedback on that work.

Benefits of Shift Left

Shifting security testing earlier in the development cycles has significant benefits in increasing the speed of feedback to developers and thereby reducing the effort required to address those issues. This is because the nearer developers are to writing the code with potential security vulnerabilities, the more familiar they will be with that code and the easier it will be for them to correct it. If developers are not notified of defects until weeks or months after they produce the code, they lose the context of the work, and it can take significantly more effort to correct.

THE COST OF TECHNICAL DEBT

People who have worked in large companies that have been around for long enough have likely encountered the impact of the increased cost of technical debt in the form of unremediated security vulnerabilities. One of the more extreme examples of this are systems that are still in production but no longer have support. On more than one occasion, I have found significant vulnerabilities in legacy systems whose developers are no longer with the company or that were developed by external companies that no longer exist.

The cost to remediate these issues requires developers who are unfamiliar with the code to go in and determine the cause of the vulnerabilities. At times, this may require significant effort to reverse-engineer these systems. In addition, because of the age and lack of knowledge about these systems, any changes may introduce significant risk to the stability of the system. Clearly, being able to address and remediate these risks at the time of development would be significantly less costly and less risky.

The data supporting this paradigm has been known for quite some time. A study by Walter Baziuk in 1995 showed that the cost of repairing a defect in production could be up to 880 times as expensive as the cost of fixing a defect at the requirements phase.[15] A study in 2002 from the National Institute of Standards & Technology (NIST) stated that the cost to fix defects after product release was 30 times that of defects found at the requirements phase.[16] In Smith's original writing on the topic of Shift Left testing, he writes, "Bugs are cheap when caught young. You can catch bugs earlier by making QA a part of your development, not just part of the release process." The same concept applies to security defects and is critical as you look at DevSecOps. If you can include security earlier in the development process, you produce secure code while reducing the time and effort to do so. At the same time, Jones found that significantly more defects were introduced at the beginning of the development cycle, which makes sense in waterfall, as this is where the bulk of the development is done. However, it means that doing testing earlier has significant implications for reducing the cost of developing and delivering secure products and services (see Figure 2.7).

Several challenges arise with the delay of defect removal in addition to the time and cost to remediate. Frequently the people needed for testing and remediation may be significantly reduced once products have been completed, especially products that have been completed for extended periods of time. Defects found later in the development cycle may also require significant re-architecture or rework. In addition, when you look at security defects, the longer these vulnerabilities are in a product, the longer the company is at risk.

Agile and DevOps amplify the opportunities for Shift Left practices because of their focus on small batch delivery and automation.

---

[15] Baziuk, Walter. "BNR/NORTEL: Path to Improve Product Quality, Reliability and Customer Satisfaction." Proceedings of Sixth International Symposium on Software Reliability Engineering. ISSRE'95, (1995): pp.256-262. Accessed May 31, 222. https://doi.org/10.1109/ISSRE.1995.497665.
[16] "Planning Report 02-3 The Economic Impacts of Inadequate Infrastructure for Software Testing." (2002). Accessed May 31, 2022.

Continuous integration and continuous deployment processes, which allow for small batch delivery, mean that there is always a working product that can be tested. In addition, because the build pipeline is automated, it necessitates automated testing. However, security issues are all too often left out of this process, introducing risk into production environments and sacrificing significant potential for reducing the cost of security. By introducing tools for SCA, SAST, and DAST, you can automatically inject security into your deployment pipeline. These tools and many more are discussed in more detail in Chapter 5, "DevSecOps Technology."

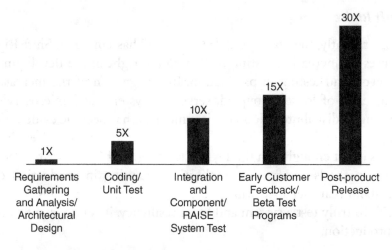

Figure 2.7 The NIST 2002 study "The Economic Impacts of Inadequate Infrastructure for Software Testing" shows that the cost of fixing defects grows substantially through later stages of the development cycles.

Smearing Left

Shifting left is not just taking the same task and doing it earlier, but doing it as early as possible, which may mean that some smaller sections can be done earlier. Dave Stanke, developer relations engineer at Google, coined the phrase *smearing left* to describe this phenomenon.[17] In the "Devopedia" post on Shift Left, the authors note that "Shift Left doesn't mean 'shifting' the position of a task within a process flow.

---

[17] Stephens, Rachel. "Developer Experience Is Security." RedMonk. February 17, 2022. https://redmonk.com/rstephens/2022/02/17/devex-is-security.

It also doesn't imply that no testing is done just before a release. It should be seen as 'spreading' the task and its concerns to all stages of the process flow. It's about continuous involvement and feedback."[18] It is obvious that penetration testing cannot be done before the application is built, but that doesn't mean all security testing must wait until the full product is built. Because you are taking the security testing typically done at the end of the cycle and spreading it toward the beginning, "smearing left" may be a more accurate way of thinking about it than "shifting left."

Shift Right

More recently, the concept of "Shift Right" has emerged. Shift Right focuses on increasing testing further to the right in the development life cycle and testing in production. In recognition of the increasing complexity of loosely coupled, serverless systems and microservices running in distributed cloud environments, it has become evident that simply testing in preproduction and other "production-like" environments is not enough. On the Dynatrace blog, Saif Gunja writes, "Shift Right methods ensure that applications running in production can withstand real user load while ensuring the same high levels of quality."[19] To truly test a system and build resiliency, it is important to test in production.

Practices like Chaos Testing, discussed in more detail in Chapter 4, "DevSecOps Process," inject failure conditions into production to ensure that production systems are resilient to such failures. Other practices—such as A/B testing and canary releases—allow you to perform tests in production to see which variants of products perform the best.

- A/B testing releases two different versions of a piece of software to test which performs better.

- Canary releases, on the other hand, release an updated version of the software to a small portion of the user population to see how it performs before releasing to all users.

[18] Padmanabhan, Arvind. "Shift Left." Devopedia. February 15, 2022. https://devopedia.org/shift-left.

[19] Gunja, Saif. "Shift Left Vs Shift Right: A DevOps Mystery Solved." Devopedia. October 27, 2022. www.dynatrace.com/news/blog/what-is-shift-left-and-what-is-shift-right.

These methods offer ways of testing in production, in effect, shifting the testing to the right in the development life cycle. Shift Right helps to get additional insight into performance of a system under real-world conditions. In addition to testing the resilience of the code, Shift Right allows you to exercise your instrumentation to ensure that these anomalies (and any potentially adverse impacts to the customers) are identified.

Shift Left for DevSecOps

The concept of Shift Left was originally applied to testing methodology, but it is key to many DevSecOps practices. Shift Left underpins many of the DevSecOps practices explored in this book. In addition, Shift Left is facilitated by the CI/CD process central to DevOps.

Shift Left fundamentally underpins one of the core concepts of DevSecOps, the concept that security is everyone's responsibility. Shifting left enables developers to take a more active role in security. Instead of a security team providing gates at the end of the cycle to prevent security vulnerabilities from getting into production systems, security is integrated into every step of the process and everything you do. Fundamentally, security must be everyone's responsibility and part of everything you do, not an afterthought to be tested at the end of the process or, worse yet, ignored altogether. Doing security testing closer to the development work shortens the feedback loops and lowers the cost to address any defects.

Shift Left fundamentally underpins one of the core concepts of DevSecOps, the concept that security is everyone's responsibility.

CONCLUSION

As the security landscape continues to evolve, so too must the response. With the continuing expansion and dilution of the network perimeter, it is no longer possible to simply provide a tight security perimeter. Zero Trust and Defense in Depth provide models that help deal with these new challenges, but they do not provide comprehensive answers to the needs of the modern enterprise.

The speed of delivery and proliferation of today's applications presents an exponential increase in cybersecurity challenges. DevSecOps provides a new model to help address the evolving security landscape, enabling developers to secure their internal systems and their customer-facing systems. By inserting security into the deployment pipelines, developers help ensure that the applications they are delivering meet the security requirements that modern customers demand. Not only that, but DevSecOps allows them to do so without delaying the rapid, and continuous, delivery of new services and features that today's customers have come to expect.

CHAPTER 3

DevSecOps People

INTRODUCTION

People are at the core of DevSecOps. While tools and processes can help enable DevSecOps, it is, more than anything, about people. DevSecOps requires a cultural transformation with people at its core. When Gene Kim (author of *The Phoenix Project: A Novel about IT, DevOps, and Helping Your Business Win*, and one of the foremost thought leaders in DevOps) first began writing about DevOps, he described it as a cultural movement. The tools and the process can reinforce that cultural transformation, but it must be, first and foremost, about the people and the underpinning cultural transformation of the workplace.

Of course, people are also the most difficult thing to change. It is relatively easy to buy and implement a new security tool. In comparison, getting security professionals, developers, and end users to behave differently is difficult. It is also important to keep in mind that security professionals have spent their careers mitigating risk. They have chosen careers focused on keeping others safe. In many cases, the safest thing to do is nothing at all. So, it is not surprising that the security community can often be change-resistant. This explains, in many instances, why security teams can be late adopters or even laggards when it comes to adopting new ways of working (see Figure 3.1). Security personnel often are slow to adopt because early adoption carries a high risk. Regardless of domain, changing the way people work is significantly more challenging than changing the technology they are using, and yet it is, arguably, the most crucial element of DevSecOps success.

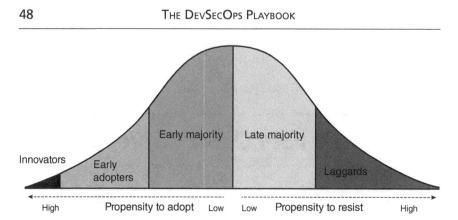

Figure 3.1 Security professionals often fall into the later stages of the innovation adoption life cycle.

COLLABORATION AT THE CORE

DevSecOps is, fundamentally, a transformation away from siloed activity and toward collaboration. As defined earlier, it is "a method of delivering value to customers based on Lean principles and *collaboration*." Collaboration is the key underpinning principle.

In its blog article on DevSecOps Culture, the security company Synk writes, "DevSecOps culture focuses on uniting the normally siloed roles of Development, Security, and Operations into a collaborative shared-responsibility paradigm. It seeks to break down barriers of finger pointing and deflection. Instead, it aims to build empathy and common goals among various disciplines within the organization."[1] In bringing people together, you focus on building collaboration and, through this, begin to build a better security organization.

> *Frequently, when I am asked a question about DevSecOps, I substitute the word collaboration in my head and, by and large, this brings me to the right answer. For example, if someone were to ask, "What is the best step to drive DevSecOps?" I think, "What is the best step to drive collaboration for security?" and the answer becomes self-evident.*

[1] "DevSecOps Culture." Snyk. March 19, 2020. https://snyk.io/series/devsecops/culture.

DevSecOps

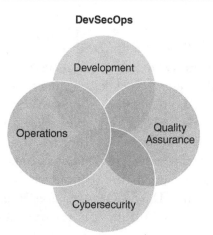

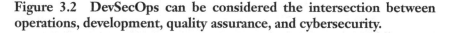

Figure 3.2 DevSecOps can be considered the intersection between operations, development, quality assurance, and cybersecurity.

The critical component of the Venn diagram of DevSecOps from Chapter 1, "Introducing DevSecOps," is the section of overlap of the different domains (see Figure 3.2). Any of the nonoverlapping domains are just the domains themselves as they have existed for many years. The critical component is the point of overlap because this is where collaboration happens.

This is one of the reasons so many people are passionate about DevSecOps. What they find through DevSecOps is that, by working together better, they can drive better security *and* faster delivery to their customers. Balancing feature delivery against security concerns is a problem that technologists have struggled with for many years. The fundamental question is, "How do you deliver securely without slowing down delivery?" And the answer, it turns out, is collaboration.

DevSecOps Culture

While collaboration is at the core of DevSecOps, there are many other elements of DevSecOps culture that are of critical importance for success. A DevOps culture includes trust, transparency, empowerment, and continuous learning. All of these cultural elements can be leveraged to build stronger security for the business.

Trust

Trust is key to DevSecOps culture but often a challenging area for security practitioners. While security is focused on protecting against threat actors with presumed malicious intent, you must, ultimately, have trust if you are going to work within an organization. In reality, you do this every day. When your co-worker asks for help with a project, you trust that they are doing the project for the company, and you trust that your help will aid in that effort. In fact, companies work only because of an assumed trust between individuals and systems within that company. DevSecOps requires tighter collaboration between teams, and this, in turn, requires trust. This is why it is so critical to build team trust, because better trust leads to better collaboration, and better collaboration leads to better business outcomes.

Build team trust, because better trust leads to better collaboration, and better collaboration leads to better business outcomes.

This is not to say you should provide blanket trust. If someone was to ask you for a complete list of your passwords, you might be a little suspicious, and for good reason! However, this does mean you should assume good intent from your teammates.

All too often when there is a security breach we jump to the assignment of blame. The reality is that most people come to work with the intention of doing the best job they can. By the same token, no one comes to work thinking, "Gee, I wonder how I can cause a major security breach today." We cite "human error" as the cause of the problem, forgetting systems in which that human error occurred. Sidney Dekker, professor of human factors and flight safety and director of research at the School of Aviation, Lund University, Sweden, writes about this extensively in his book *The Field Guide to Understanding Human Error*. This tendency to look for individual blame erodes trust, which is so essential to building a strong team. Dekker writes, "Getting rid of Bad Apples tends to send a signal to other people to be more careful with what they do, say, report, or disclose. It does not make 'human errors' go away, but does tend to make the evidence of them go away; evidence that might otherwise have been available to you and your organization so that you could learn and improve."[2]

Building collaboration and trust between team members has become ever more challenging during the COVID-19 pandemic and the increase of remote workforces. With increasing numbers of tech workers working from home, people are increasingly detached from their teams and have fewer social interactions, which are vital to building relationships and trust. One of the things you lose with increasingly remote and hybrid teams is the opportunity to build trust between team members. When all interactions occur via video conferencing, they become increasingly transactional, leaving little room for the sort of interactions that build strong, trust-based relationships. However, you can take steps to increase trust on a team, including these:

- **Create opportunities for teams to meet face-to-face**—It is important to be purposeful about creating opportunities for people to come together face-to-face and, when that happens, encourage interactions that are focused on team building and understanding one another. When you build empathy for others, when you understand where others are coming from, it helps to build trust. As you look at building teams in remote and hybrid models, it is critical that you think about the value of working together and how you bring that value to teams that do not share the same office space.

- **Be open and honest about failure**—It is important that people understand that we all fail at times and that this is acceptable, especially when we are open about it and learn from it. In the Spencer Stuart blog, James M. Citrin and Darleen Derosa state, "A sure sign of a lack of trust is the blame game: team members pointing the finger at others for problems or failures and no one taking accountability. Leaders can emphasize the importance of being open and honest by inviting team members to regularly share their challenges as well as their successes."[3] It is especially critical for leaders to model this behavior for others. By showing

[2] Dekker, Sidney. 2014. The Field Guide to Understanding 'Human Error'. 3rd ed. Burlington: Ashgate Publishing Ltd.

[3] Citrin, James M., and Darleen Derosa. "No Trust, No Team: Six Best Practices for Building Trust on Virtual Teams." SpencerStuart. March 24, 2021. www.spencer stuart.com/leadership-matters/2021/march/no-trust-no-team.

that we are all susceptible to error and that there is no recrimination for making errors, we begin to build a learning culture.

Building Trust Through Phishing Campaigns

When Wiley first launched their internal phishing campaign, users were hesitant to report suspicious emails. The security team sent fake phishing emails to users and tracked the number of users who clicked the link and the number who clicked "Report Phishing activity." Users at first were afraid to report phishing emails for fear of being wrong.

As users began to see that clicking the button to report phish had no negative consequence, even if they were incorrect, they began to see that it was okay to make a mistake. This also encouraged users to report when they accidentally clicked real phishing emails.

- **Be truthful**—This may sound obvious, but it is often overlooked for the sake of expediency. Not only is it important to be honest, but it is important to follow through on promises made. If you are consistently truthful and consistently live up to your promises, it will inspire trust throughout the team.

- **Be empathetic**—Simply asking your colleagues how they are doing ensures they know you care about them on a personal level. In addition, it may help you better understand where they are coming from. In an increasingly disconnected world, building empathy into an organization can go a long way.

Building Empathy Among Colleagues

Wiley launched a "Check In on a Colleague" initiative. They encouraged people across the company to take some time out of their workday to check in with a colleague. Whether it was

(continues)

(*continued*)

going to lunch, grabbing coffee, or setting up some time to chat over Teams, people found ways to connect. These activities helped give all employees the opportunity to connect with their fellow Wiley employees, thereby building connection and trust between team members.

Numerous studies have found a correlation between intra-team trust and performance. An analysis across 55 different studies on the relationship found "[t]eam trust was positively correlated with team performance. . .higher levels of trust in business teams are generally associated with higher levels of team performance."[4] Given the strong relationship between team trust and team performance and the challenges arising from an increasingly global hybrid work environment, it is essential that you look for ways to build trust between security teams and the rest of the organization.

Transparency

Transparency is another key to DevSecOps culture, and it is also an important way to build trust. It is important that you share data as much as possible without risking the security of your systems. This applies to transparency of your business plans as well as transparency in your data. If you can share data in your company, it provides a better chance that you can identify security issues and resolve them more quickly.

This is, of course, a bit of a nuanced subject when it comes to cybersecurity where transparency can actually increase your risk. You obviously cannot be transparent about implementation details of your cyber defenses, as an attacker may use this information to breach your systems. However, we are increasingly seeing that being open and

---

[4] Morrissette, Amy M., and Jennifer L. Kisamore. "Trust and Performance in Business Teams: A Meta-analysis." Team Performance Management: An International Journal 26, no. 5/6 (2020): 287–300. Accessed June 11, 2023. https://doi.org/10.1108/TPM-02-2020-0012

transparent has positive results, even when it comes to cybersecurity. In a survey by Deloitte of people who received a breach notification, they found that "34 percent said they trusted that organization more. In addition, 73 percent of this cohort who received a privacy breach notification did not trust the organization any less following the notification."[5] This is not to say that transparency means exposing everything at all times—you must still be judicious in what you share—but, in sharing, you have the opportunity to build trust and a culture of collaboration that drives better business results.

Transparency can take many forms and can be as simple as a meeting to share business direction. It can also take the form of anonymized data shared across teams to drive better business decisions. It can also take the form of sharing data between companies to drive governmental action against cybercriminals. We are increasingly seeing this sort of industry-wide data sharing to help all companies be better prepared for the next attack.

THE SHARED RESPONSIBILITY MODEL

As DevSecOps focuses on collaboration, you must create a model of shared responsibilities where everyone is responsible for security. If you are developing a product, you are responsible for the security of the product. If you are implementing a new network design, you are responsible for the security of that network. If you are implementing a new tool, you are responsible for the security of that tool. In DevSecOps it is no longer acceptable to simply assume that the security team will take care of security for you. For DevSecOps to be successful, you must break the pattern of simply throwing the responsibility over the wall to another group.

It is not sufficient to simply say "everyone is responsible now" because that diffusion of responsibilities can lead to a situation where no one takes ownership or accountability.

However, this change can create complications in defining who exactly is responsible for specific tasks. It is not sufficient to simply say

---

[5] "Transparency Builds Trust." Deloitte. Accessed June 11, 2023. www2.deloitte.com/au/en/pages/financial-services/articles/transparency-builds-trust.html.

"everyone is responsible now" because that diffusion of responsibilities can lead to a situation where no one takes ownership or accountability. Who, for example, is responsible for defining security standards? Who, specifically, is monitoring for security alerts? Who, specifically, is coordinating customer communication in case of a data breach?

Ownership

It is important to recognize that the idea of "ownership," while conceptually simple, is often more complex and requires another level of thought and consideration. Often people bandy about the idea of ownership, asking, "Who owns this (process/task/application/infrastructure/ etc.)?" The reality is often more complex as many people are involved in the care, management, and completion of a given task.

One way to address this ambiguity is through the use of *RACI matrices*. RACI matrices detail every task in a given process and define who is Responsible, Accountable, Consulted, and Informed (RACI) for each one. This forces you to delineate just what is meant by "ownership" and detail all the activities involved in a given process. With a RACI approach, the responsible party does the work. The Accountable party may be the same or different from the Responsible party, but this person is ultimately held accountable for ensuring completion of the tasks. In addition, with a RACI approach, only one party may hold the Accountability for a given task. This ensures that, while there may be many people involved in completing a given task, there is ultimately only one person who is held accountable for that task is completed.

That said, the absence of a RACI model should not dissuade you from taking ownership. Ultimately, a RACI model is just a tool to aid and clarify ownership. Everyone must work together to be clear about who is responsible, and a RACI is one way to do this.

I often think of baseball outfielders when there is a fly ball and it is unclear who should catch it. Everyone wants to make sure that the ball is caught and, if it is not clear who should catch it, one person should call out "Got it" so that they do not run head on into the other outfielders. What matters in this situation is that all people want to solve the problem together, and they communicate about who will be doing what, both beforehand and during, to ensure optimal outcomes.

In a DevSecOps model, while there may be different people responsible for implementing the solution, the application team must ultimately be accountable for the security and performance of the system. It is no longer the case that one team will build a system and the security team will still be held accountable for its security. In a 2022 article in *Computer Weekly*, Mandy Andress wrote, "DevSecOps is a mindset and way of working within the application security field in which security is a part of everyone's job, not just one team. . .organizations should consider delegating responsibility for DevSecOps to engineering teams, not security teams."[6]

In many DevSecOps implementations, the security team may still be accountable for providing the framework, tools, and governance for the rest of the organization, but it is the development teams themselves who are accountable for ensuring the security of the systems they are building. In this way, the teams work together in a well-defined manner to ensure the overall security of the organization. By sharing the responsibility for security, you ensure that you build security into everything you do, and you get security closer to the source of the problem, which leads to more secure products and services.

Accountability

While trust is a key element of the DevSecOps culture, this does not mean there should be an absence of accountability. In fact, a trust-based culture should mean that expectations around accountability are even higher. The lack of micromanagement and oversight is, in fact, dependent on the assumption that everyone is responsible for delivering on their promises. To be part of a community based on trust, we must all be accountable for our actions and delivery of our promises.

If a problem occurs, it is important to be open and honest with the role one plays in the problem. In an environment that is not blame based, being open about our own failures becomes easier. If there is truly no fear of retribution and instead a focus on learning, being open about failure becomes a learning opportunity. If people are having

---

[6] Andress, Mandy. "It's Time for Engineering Teams to Own DevSecOps." ComputerWeekly.Com. September 23, 2022. www.computerweekly.com/opinion/Its-time-for-engineering-teams-to-own-DevSecOps.

problems being open about mistakes, it is important to consider whether you are somehow instilling a culture of fear or retribution. Employee engagement surveys and management 360s are useful in understanding the cultural environment. That said, the very fact that people are hesitant to share information openly about their failures may be indicative of a culture of fear.

It may be difficult to set security as a top-level goal if upper management is not genuinely security focused. While security is increasingly becoming a topic for boards and executives, some companies still see security as a cost that must be paid but without a real understanding of the criticality. In these instances, it is often useful to keep in mind that cybersecurity breaches are one of the few things that can cost C-level executives their jobs. In 2013, the data breach of the retail giant Target cost CEO Greg Steinhafel his job, and in 2014 the Sony Pictures breach led to the resignation of Board Co-Chairman Amy Pascal.[7] These are just two of a growing number of examples of how cybersecurity has an impact, not just on the company but also on executives responsible for the company. What is more important here is that, by including security in shared goals, it becomes part of everyone's responsibilities.

A shared responsibility model can also be fostered by building shared goals for the organization. Goals should include security at the highest levels of the organization. And these goals should cascade down throughout the organization. By setting these goals at the top levels of the organization, you set the north star toward which the entire company is pointed and ensure security is part of everything you do.

The Role of the Security Team

With shared responsibility and collaboration around security, the role of the security team must fundamentally change. With DevSecOps, the security team is no longer a policing organization responsible for ensuring that everyone is following the rules and punishing rule breakers. Instead, the role of the security team must shift to governance and guidance.

[7] NeSmith, Brian. "CEOs: The Data Breach Is Your Fault." Forbes. June 26, 2018. www.forbes.com/sites/forbestechcouncil/2018/06/26/ceos-the-data-breach-is-your-fault/?sh=71cfd658b0f7.

With shared responsibility and collaboration around security, the role of the security team must fundamentally change.

The modern security team should focus on developing the standards and governance around security and designing systems to automatically monitor, measure, and enforce these rules. By integrating security directly into the tools that developers use to build and deliver products, security becomes integrated into the way teams work. Instead of a policing organization, security teams are partners to development, operations, and SRE teams, helping them drive best practices and deliver secure products.

PSYCHOLOGICAL SAFETY

For a DevOps culture to thrive, people must have psychological safety. The concept of psychological safety first emerged in 1965 in the book *Personal and Organizational Change Through Group Methods: The Laboratory Approach* by Edgar Schein and Warren Bennis, who describe it as "an atmosphere where one can take chances (which experimentalism implies) without fear and with sufficient protection."[8] Part of empowering engineers is developing trust, and a trust-based culture requires psychological safety. Harvard Business School professor Dr. Amy C. Edmondson expanded on the concept, describing it as "a belief that one will not be punished or humiliated for speaking up with ideas, questions, concerns, or mistakes." However, this term has taken on increasing importance as we look at building collaboration, empowerment, and a learning culture. You must build a culture where people feel safe if you are to encourage learning and empower engineers.

Psychological safety is the fourth ideal identified in Gene Kim's book *The Unicorn Project*. In describing the psychological safety, Kim says, "No one will take risks, experiment, or innovate in a culture of fear, where people are afraid to tell the boss bad news."[9] When people are

---

[8] Schein, Edgar H., and Warren G. Bennis. "Personal And Organizational Change Through Group Meth Ods: The Laboratory Approach." Adult Education 17, no. 2 (1967). Accessed June 11, 2023. https://doi.org/10.1177/074171366701700211.

[9] Kim, Gene. 2019. The Unicorn Project: A Novel About Developers, Digital Disruption, and Thriving in the Age of Data. Oregon: IT Revolution.

focused overly on mistake prevention rather than value creation, they often do the minimal work needed, reducing output for the company.

In her TEDx talk called "Building a Psychologically Safe Workplace," Amy Edmondson provided three suggestions for fostering a culture of psychological safety.

- Frame the work as a learning problem, not an execution problem.

- Acknowledge your own fallibility.

- Model curiosity.[10]

Transparency and honesty help build an environment of psychological safety and trust. The best leaders are the ones who respect problem analysis because it ultimately saves everybody time and money. Trust and physiological safety, in turn, build an environment where teams can feel empowered and a learning culture can develop—this sort of culture is essential to DevSecOps.

Empowerment

Empowering engineers is another key component of DevSecOps culture. Engineers who are empowered by their managers deliver better results. This sort of empowerment is often created through trust-based cultures.

By instilling trust in engineers, they will be empowered to deliver their best work. Engineers are, by and large, highly educated and highly compensated professions. It is a safe assumption that these people are trying to do their best work. If you start by trusting that people are trying their best, it helps you empower them.

This approach represents a fundamental shift in how you approach management of people. Using the same approach to manage highly skilled engineers as one would to manage low skilled assembly line workers does not make sense and has a negative impact on

---

[10] Edmondson, Amy. "Building a Psychologically Safe Workplace." TEDx Talks. May 5, 2014. Video, www.youtube.com/watch?v=LhoLuui9gX8.

productivity. Unfortunately, many common management practices today are based on the bureaucratic, tightly controlled management practices developed for managing large groups of low-skilled employees. Instead of managing engineers such as assembly line workers, it is important to approach them like doctors or lawyers, understanding the immense knowledge they have and empowering them to act independently based on that knowledge.

When leaders micromanage employees or are quick to blame them for errors, those employees tend to do less work than they might otherwise. Examining every piece of work and being quick to criticize creates a culture of fear where people do not strive to do their best but, instead, try only not to make mistakes.

This approach has interesting implications to questions about work-from-home policies in the post-COVID-19 workforce. Companies that truly empower workers allow them to work wherever and whenever they want, trusting that they will know how best to manage their time and effort to produce the best and most work. Forcing employees to come into the office clearly sends a message that "We do not trust you to do your jobs unless we are watching you do your work." When this happens, we have to wonder why companies would be hiring people and paying them large sums of money if they cannot trust them to do their jobs independently. Either they have hired the wrong people or they have not built a culture that inspires people to do their best.

Ultimately what is important about highly skilled workforces is delivery. There are still deadlines that must be met and security standards that must be adhered to, but if people are delivering high-quality work on time, where and when that work is done is less important. And, by and large, if managers trust and empower their employees, those employees will deliver better results.

This is not to say that there isn't value to working together in the same physical location but rather that it is important to understand what that value of in-person work is and to understand motives and desired outcomes when determining how and when engineers must come to the office. Setting values for human contact and creating events that require in-office bonding needs to be part of how employees work. At the same time, letting employees know that they are trusted to choose when and where they do their work goes a long way to empowering them to do their best.

Learning Culture

Trust and empowerment go a long way to building a learning culture, which is another key component of DevSecOps. A learning culture is open to change and continually learning. One of the most successful ways to institute a learning culture is to ensure it is embedded in the day-to-day activities and processes that make the business flow.

For cybersecurity you can build a learning culture throughout the daily life with activities such as these:

- **Incident postmortems**—Incident postmortems are an opportunity to review an incident after it has been resolved. By focusing on learning rather than blame, incident postmortems can provide an excellent opportunity to embed a learning culture into daily activity of a company. See Chapter 4, "DevSecOps Process," for additional information about incident postmortems.

- **Tabletop exercises**—Tabletop exercises allow the team to walk through theoretical cybersecurity incidents and discuss actions that all parties involved would take in response. This provides an opportunity to identify potential gaps and learn from other team members to build better coordination and better responses.

- **Game days**—Game days simulate a cybersecurity event such as an attack or breach to practice the team's response and learn and improve. Game days are similar to tabletop exercises except that game days involve real-world simulation and response, while tabletop exercises are discussion-based without use of actual systems.

- **Phishing campaigns**—Phishing campaigns are a tool for sending simulated phishing emails to a company's employees to test the ability to identify and respond. Running these on a regular cadence is an excellent method to train company's users to identify and report potentially suspicious emails.

As phishing is one of the top cybersecurity attack vectors, this can be an important tool.

- **Training**—Continual training is another critical aspect of any cybersecurity program. As people/social engineering are one of the most common paths to breaches, it is critical that you continually work to increase security knowledge throughout the organization. It is critical to develop a comprehensive training program for all people in a company. One should determine what training is required for employees based on their role within the company. Many of the standard trainings are applicable to all employees. It is also critical to recognize that training is not a one-time activity. It is not enough to do a training for new hires; trainings must be revised and repeated on a regular basis.

- **Cross training**—In addition to standard training practices, it can be hugely valuable to have people cross-train in areas outside of their own. This can be a powerful method of building a well-rounded team as it helps build breadth of knowledge. In addition to building skills, cross-training is an excellent method for building a DevSecOps culture, as it provides people with insight into the work that others are doing and thereby builds empathy and opens opportunities for cross-team collaboration.

BUILDING CYBERSECURITY INTO THE CULTURE

At Wiley, every October is Cybersecurity Month: a full month dedicated to cybersecurity awareness and education. This month includes activities like capture the flag—team-based events designed to test the cybersecurity skills of the teams by discovering hidden "flags" within intentionally vulnerable systems—and red team/blue team events. It also includes trainings, trivia competitions, brown bags, and even a Halloween dress-up-as-your-favorite-vulnerability-or-exploit competition! This is another example of how Wiley builds cybersecurity learning into the culture.

Part of building a learning culture is embracing failure as a learning opportunity. In *The Unicorn Project*, Gene Kim describes, "The corrosive effects that a culture of fear creates, where mistakes are routinely punished and scapegoats fired. Punishing failure and 'shooting the messenger' only cause people to hide their mistakes, and eventually, all desire to innovate is completely extinguished."

It is important to note that some of our most successful engineers are the ones making the most mistakes. This is because it is precisely those engineers who are doing the most work, taking on the hardest tasks, driving innovation, and taking risks. These mistakes are often an indicator of people who are pushing the envelope of what we can do with technology. You need to reward such innovation instead of punishing mistakes.

Mistakes occur only in a system that allows for those mistakes to occur. Sidney Deker notes this, writing "the apparent simplicity of 'human error' is misleading. Underneath every seemingly obvious, simple story of error, there is a second, deeper story. . . . This second story is inevitably an organizational story, a story about the system in which people work, about its management, technology, governance, administration and operation." It is crucial, when looking at errors or mistakes, that you look at the system as a whole and search for opportunities to improve in all areas.

It is critical to embrace mistakes as a learning opportunity. This is an important part of building a learning culture. When, not if, mistakes happen, it is important not to seek out the individual responsible and to punish but rather to understand all of the elements that contributed to that failure and learn from it and grow stronger. The most critical thing that can happen when mistakes occur is that the organization, as a whole, must learn. This is even more important than correcting the causes of the mistake. And, there are often many.

Incident Postmortems

Incidents offer a unique opportunity to build a learning culture. By taking the time to learn from errors that cause security incidents, you build learning into your daily work. But how these are approached is critical to building a learning culture. These cannot be approached as an exercise to fill out a form. These also cannot be approached as an exercise to find out what the root cause was and apply a fix. These approaches are too myopic and miss the opportunity to learn and grow as an organization. It is important in these reviews to first truly understand what happened from every person's perspective who participated. By understanding what each person was thinking and what lead to the decisions, you can begin to build an empathetic and learning organization. Only then can or should you begin to identify improvement opportunities or actions that should be taken. Additional details on incident postmortems can be found in Chapter 4.

Security Training Programs

Security training programs are a critical part of the learning culture around cybersecurity. It is critical that they not be limited to a single type or method of training. It is also important that these be embedded into a regular cadence, repeated at intervals and, in some cases, integrated on an ongoing basis. Training should also be catered to the people responsible for training.

Every cybersecurity training program will differ based on the organization. Requirements will differ based on size, complexity, potential threats, industry, and compliance requirements for that business or industry. The first step in developing a comprehensive cybersecurity program is to assess the key threats to the organization as compliance requirements.

Training programs can include new-hire training, annual compliance training for any in-scope compliance requirements such as the *Payment Card Industry (PCI) standard* for those companies accepting credit cards or *Sarbanes-Oxley (SOX)* for companies in the public domain, and ongoing knowledge testing such as phishing tests. It is also important to understand the various stakeholders of a cybersecurity training program. You must train end users in security best practices while also providing specialized training for the security professionals in your organization. It is important to provide basic training to all end users of a company to ensure they understand the threats that are faced.

Specific groups of users may require specialized or additional training, such as executives who may be at heightened risk levels due to their elevated position within the companies. Training for security professionals within the company provides an excellent opportunity to invest in internal resources and build the strength of the security team, while improving employee retention. Offering training and certifications for your security team can be a great way to help motivate your workforce while strengthening your security posture.

INTEGRATED PHISHING TESTS INTO YOUR TRAINING PROGRAM

Wiley uses tools to do regular phishing tests. According to the 2022 Verizon Data Breach Investigation Report, phishing is the second highest risk entry path to exploiting a company's environment, so it is critical not only that they have tools to protect automatically but also that users are trained to identify and react to potential phishing threats.

Every couple of weeks, a test phishing campaign is sent to the entire organization. People who click the link are given feedback and direct training on the spot about how to identify phishing emails. People who correctly identify and click the Phish Alert Report button are given positive reinforcement. For people who make repeated mistakes, additional training and support are provided.

In addition, Wiley leverages the data on a global basis to identify regions or teams that are performing well and others that may need additional support. By running these sorts of test campaigns on a continuous basis, they ensure that there is a constant awareness of the security threats present through email.

Whatever the audience for security training, there are several things you can do to ensure that your security training is successful. It is important to develop training that is interactive and engaging. To that end, make sure that the training is relevant to the audience you are targeting. Make sure the content for the training is relatable to the people taking the training. The more engaging you can make the training, the better the results for the entire organization.

ORGANIZING FOR DevSecOps

If DevSecOps is focused on collaboration, it is critical then that you build organizational structures that facilitate collaboration. When thinking about how to organize teams most effectively for DevSecOps, you can take learnings from DevOps, which has matured in many organizations far more than DevSecOps.

It is important to understand that there is no one right way to organize DevSecOps. While organizational structures may vary, what matters is that they enable the DevOps principles of collaboration and fewer hand-offs. Phrasing the question around "collaboration," the question "How do I organize for collaboration on security?" seems to miss the point to some extent. There is obviously no one way to organize for collaboration, and, in fact, the organization is going to be secondary to the culture. That is, if collaboration is built into your culture, many different organizational structures can help build on that collaboration. The opposite is also true—if a culture of collaboration is not there, organizational structure alone will not fix that. Not only that, but there is a low likelihood that an alternative organizational structure will be made in a company that does not have collaboration built in.

In their popular blog post, "DevOps Topologies," Matthew Skelton and Manuel Pais discuss many of the different organizational patterns and anti-patterns for DevOps in which they state, "The DevOps Topologies reflect two key ideas: (1) There is no one-size-fits-all approach to structuring teams for DevOps success. The suitability and effectiveness of any given topology depends on the organization's context. (2) There are several topologies known to be detrimental (anti-patterns) to DevOps success, as they overlook or go against core tenets of DevOps."[11] The Skelton and Pais post goes on to describe several common patterns to organize for DevOps including dev and ops collaboration, fully shared ops responsibilities, and ops as infrastructure as a service (platform). They also point to several anti-patterns, including dev and ops silos and DevOps team silo.

Skelton and Pais go on to say that "Organizations must design teams intentionally by asking these questions: Given our skills, constraints, cultural and engineering maturity, desired software architecture, and business goals, which team topology will help us deliver results faster and safer? How can we reduce or avoid handovers between teams in the main flow of change? Where should the boundaries be in the software system in order to preserve system viability and encourage rapid flow? How can our teams align to that?"[12]

That said, there are several organizational structures that can aid DevSecOps and some that may be detrimental. In fact, the anti-patterns or organizational patterns that deter collaboration may be more impactful. One of the most obvious is the organization around siloed specialty groups such as security or operations. As with other areas, security teams have lagged in adopting new organizational structures. In many companies, security remains a siloed team operating fully independent of other teams. In *The DevOps Handbook*, Gene, Humble, Debois, and Willis write, "When infosec is organized as a silo outside of development and operations, many problems arise."[13]

It is important to note that the organizational structure for DevSecOps will depend on many elements, including the size of the company, the maturity of the DevSecOps program, and the complexity, and age, of the tech stack. For example, it is much easier for a small startup built on modern technologies to do DevOps than a large company with a variety of technologies dating back to the 1980s.

---

[11] Skelton, Matthew, and Manuel Pais. "What Team Structure Is Right for DevOps to Flourish?" DevOps Topologies. Accessed June 11, 2023. https://web.devops topologies.com.

[12] Skelton, Matthew, and Manuel Pais. 2018. Team Topologies: Organizing Business and Technology Teams for Fast Flow. Oregon: IT Revolution.

[13] Kim, Gene, Jez Humble, Patrick Debois, and John Willis. 2021. The DevOps Handbook: How to Create World-Class Agility, Reliability, & Security in Technology Organizations. 1st ed. Portland: IT Revolution Press.

DevOps ORIENTATION OF SMALLER COMPANIES

I often joke that when I ran technology for a small startup back during the tech bubble of the 1990s, I was doing DevOps before there was DevOps. I was leading a very small tech team, and we had to do everything, from racking and stacking servers to developing the code to getting up at 2 a.m. when things went bump in the night. Our small tech team was development, QA, operations, security, and everything in between.

The reality is that any tech team small enough to be fully self-contained is, by its nature, doing DevSecOps insomuch as they are working together to do all the parts of product development and security and operations. It is only at scale that you really see the start of specialization, which leads to the silos, which need to be broken down.

One of the most successful organizational paradigms of DevOps that you can apply to DevSecOps is the concept of the site reliability engineering team and embedded site reliability engineers. The concept of site reliability engineering originated at Google in 2003 with the idea that teams needed a role to focus efforts on the reliability of the system. In the organizational approach developed by Google, there is a core site reliability engineering team, which provides guidance, governance, frameworks, standards, and, in some cases, shared tooling. In addition, there is another part of the team of SREs embedded within other teams.

The embedded SREs focus on a deep understanding of reliability engineering as it applies to the specific product or service of the team in which they are working. This pattern fits very well for DevSecOps and can easily build on existing security teams as long as the security team is willing to work in collaboration with other teams and break out of the siloed approach. With this model, a core team provides security standards and direction to other groups looking for help. In addition, security engineers or, alternatively, security champions, are embedded within the application teams. Embedded resources can report directly to the security team or via a dotted line—the key is that they are working in conjunction with, and as an extension of, the security team.

Building a **DevSecOps** Culture

We've discussed the culture of DevSecOps as well as the type of people who comprise a strong DevSecOps culture, but how do you actually instill this culture within your company? How do you build a culture in which security is part of everything you do?

Security Champions

One great tool to use is the concept of *security champions*. A security champions program empowers SREs, developers, and quality engineers to become a champion in their teams. This person can help bridge the gap by evangelizing, managing, and enforcing the security posture while acting as an extended member of the security team.

Security champions should be voluntary and be people who desire to learn more about cybersecurity. This provides a mechanism to promote application security best practices throughout the organization. Security champions become a point of contact for security-related questions or concerns within their respective application teams. Security champion programs help improve collaboration between the security team and the rest of the organization.

These programs also provide significant benefits to those who choose to be security champions. They provide an opportunity for people who are interested in security to learn valuable new skills. The security champions gain greater visibility across the enterprise. They also build valuable cross-team and cross-organization relationships, which increase their value to the company while building the DevSecOps culture.

In addition, security champions can form a group that spans the company to enable continued learning and best practices sharing. Regular security champion meetings help build collaboration and continual learning throughout the company. Security champions programs also function as a way to drive standards and best practices across the organization. This makes the security champions a force multiplier for the security team. It is not possible, or desirable, for the security team to have a person on every team, as this would ensure that security must scale linearly with the growth of a company. By enabling all people and promoting security best practices through security champions, they can emphasize security practices without continuing to grow security staff.

Security champions help embed security into every team. This, in turn, emphasizes the idea that security is everyone's responsibility and not just the domain of a separate security team. By developing a comprehensive security champions program, you not only instantly increase the reach of the security team, but you also help build a culture of shared responsibility and continual learning.

Internal Bug Bounties

Internal security bug bounty programs offer a reward for identifying security vulnerabilities in applications or services provided by the company. These programs offer a reward for anyone who can identify security vulnerabilities in existing products. They help build security awareness while helping ensure the security of the products. Incentives can come in the form of recognition or even monetary compensation. These programs help build a culture of security through the organization by encouraging everyone to participate in the identification of security vulnerabilities.

Not only do security-related bug bounties help identify potential security issues within a company's products, but they also encourage employees to better understand the avenues an adversary might exploit and therefore become more knowledgeable about pitfalls to be avoided.

THE EVOLUTION OF THE EMPLOYEE (T-SHAPED PEOPLE)

As your technological approach evolves, so too must the type of people who you look to fill the roles. The concept of the *T-shaped* employee refers to the idea that we now look for employees who not only have a great breadth of knowledge, as represented by the vertical line in the letter *T*, but also a depth of knowledge represented by the horizontal line. The concept of the T-shaped employee has been around for quite some time now. With references dating as far back as the 1980s, the concept of the T-shaped employee was first referenced in the article "The Hunt Is On for the Renaissance Man of Computing" by David Guest in the *Independent* (September 17, 1991). However, with DevSecOps, this concept takes on increasing relevance.

This is an important concept for DevSecOps, as people must understand not only their individual domains but also the broader technical environment in which they are operating. In addition, they must understand the broader business context within which they are operating. Because DevSecOps requires all people to be responsible for security and operations, they must understand those areas as well. Developers must not only understand the programming language in which they are developing, they must also have a breadth of knowledge extending to the infrastructure they are operating on as well as the security requirements for their application.

Today, expanding the breadth of developer's knowledge to security and infrastructure is aided by abstraction and automation of these elements. For example, the use of Amazon Web Services (AWS) means that developers do not know the details of router configuration, but they must, nonetheless, still understand how to implement their service via the AWS services. This is one of the reasons it is so critical that you make security easily accessible through automation. You cannot expect every engineer to also be a security engineer, but you can expect them to be security conscious. By doing things like automating the deployment of endpoint security by embedding it in the golden AWS image, you provide the automation to easily enable security best practices and enable T-shaped employees to succeed.

This is not to say that every engineer must be a developer, DBA, network engineer, and security engineer all in one. There is certainly room for depth of knowledge in each of these fields. However, it does mean that every engineer needs to be aware of the broad spectrum of operational and security requirements in which their systems are going to operate, and they must be capable of building their systems and ensuring they continue to run in a secure way. For DevSecOps to be effective, everyone involved in the development and delivery of technical products and services must have a basic understanding of the basic security risk implications of the systems or features they are working on and must be responsible for ensuring their safety.

HIRING FOR DevSecOps

In today's job market, DevOps and security engineers are two of the most in-demand skill sets, and when you look for a combination of the two in one person, it can be next to impossible. Finding and retaining the top DevSecOps engineers is even tougher. If DevSecOps focuses on a culture of collaboration, then hiring for DevSecOps engineers means finding people not only who are good technically but, more importantly, who are good collaborators. Identifying these soft skills can be significantly harder than any technical skills, and yet it is critical. One of the reasons that collaboration is so critical to hire for is that it is easier to train someone in a new skill than it is to get them to change their behaviors.

Key Characteristics

When hiring for DevSecOps, you should focus on key characteristics, including these:

- Creative problem solving
- Communication
- Collaboration
- Curiosity

Your interview process should look for these traits in any candidate. You should structure your interviews carefully to ensure you are covering trust, collaboration, and culture aspects. Questions like the following can help illuminate practical teamwork skills:

- Tell me a time when your team had a conflict and what you did to resolve it.
- Tell me about a time when you had a conflict with your supervisor and what you did to resolve it.
- Tell me about a time a project you were working on was not going in the right direction and what you did to resolve it.

More advanced methods, such as role playing, can also be used to further illuminate a candidate's interpersonal skills in real-world scenarios. Whatever you do, it is important to ensure you illuminate the interpersonal skills and highlight those DevSecOps attributes that are critical for your company.

> One of my favorite interview questions is "Tell me how a flush toilet works." While most security engineers don't work on toilets on a regular basis, the answers can illustrate a natural curiosity. I press this handle and something happens. I wonder how that works? Beyond that, it can tell you if they've been proactive in troubleshooting a potential problem and getting their hands dirty, literally and figuratively. And, barring previous knowledge of plumbing, it tells you if they can think deductively, based on what they know about toilets and how they work.

As with any hiring, it is important that you structure your interviews well and are clear about what each of the interviewees are going to focus on to cover all aspects of a job and a candidate. One interview may focus more on the technical aspects while another may focus more on the soft skills. Because DevSecOps is such a competitive skills market, it is important to keep in mind that the candidate is evaluating your company at the same time you are evaluating them. If your process has long delays or is not well organized, you are likely to lose the best candidates. You should also make the interview process an opportunity to tell candidates about the reasons your company is a great place to work. Even if they do not end up in the position, this is an important opportunity to build the company brand in the security and engineering community.

Diversity, Equity, and Inclusion

Like other technical fields, when hiring for DevSecOps, building a diverse team can provide tremendous benefits. Not only does diversity open up additional hiring opportunities, but it also improves the performance of the team.

McKinsey & Company and PricewaterhouseCoopers (PwC) have demonstrated the measurable value diversity brings to a team.

Representing the diverse society you operate in and the customers you serve brings a greater number of ideas and speed of innovation. Having a diverse set of team members brings a broader range of viewpoints, which often leads to better solutions. A 2016 *Harvard Business Review* article noted that "non-homogenous teams are simply smarter. Working with people who are different from you may challenge your brain to overcome its stale ways of thinking and sharpen its performance."[14] Yet, according to a report by Tech Nation, just 15 percent of tech workers are from black, Asian, and minority backgrounds, and 19 percent of tech workers are women.[15]

In addition to delivering better results, hiring diverse candidates can broaden your talent pool. If you push yourself to ensure you include gender and racial diversity, there are large sources of untapped talent that you can make part of your team. By targeting these talent pools, you can find talent that competitors are missing.

However, talent diversity does not just happen. You must be intentional about hiring and building diverse teams. When hiring, it is critical that you specifically target diverse populations. Starting from talent outreach, you can look to target female and nonwhite colleges as well as other institutions. You also need to take action, such as anonymizing applicants names, to eliminate bias in the hiring process as much as possible. Once you have brought diverse candidates into your team, it is also important that you ensure the workplace environment is a comfortable and safe environment for everyone. It is also important to nourish diverse talent and ensure that people have opportunities to grow with your company.

CONCLUSION

When you look at the human aspect of DevSecOps, you need to look at how we you a culture around security. People and culture are often the most challenging parts of any transformation, so it is critical that

[14] Rock, David, and Heidi Grant. "Why Diverse Teams Are Smarter." Harvard Business Review. November 4, 2016. https://hbr.org/2016/11/why-diverse-teams-are-smarter.

[15] Browne, Orla. "What % of People Working in Tech Are from BAME Backgrounds?" Tech Nation. August 22, 2018. https://technation.io/news/what-of-people-working-in-tech-are-from-bame-backgrounds.

you do not underestimate the challenge of this aspect of DevSecOps. Changing how people behave takes time and must be ingrained into how you work. Like the security check at the beginning of the day at a construction site, it is important to develop routines that build security into daily activities for every part of the technology organization.

You can build security into your culture through security champions, activities such as game days, tabletops, red team activities, and bug bounties. But, to develop a culture of DevSecOps, it must be integrated into how you work.

It is also critical to break down silos between teams and organize in ways that help embed security into all activities. Whether that be through security champions, embedded security engineers, or shared security practice leads, the point must be emphasized that security is everyone's job.

Trust breeds empowerment, trust encourages transparency, and trust and transparency enable a learning culture.

The most critical component of DevSecOps is in building a culture around security that embraces the DevOps culture. This must be a culture built on trust, empowerment, and transparency. Ultimately, trust in each other builds empowerment. When you trust people to do the right thing, they will be empowered to take action. Trust encourages transparency because when people know they are trusted to do the right thing, they will be empowered to share what they have learned, to share what they did right, and maybe to share what they didn't. And each of these items—trust, empowerment, and transparency—leads to a learning culture that will continue to learn, grow, and thrive securely in the competitive business landscape.

CHAPTER 4

DevSecOps Process

INTRODUCTION

DevSecOps as a set of principles, and a newer one at that, does not have any inherent processes. These principles provide underlying guidance around the tools and practices within DevSecOps, but they do not provide step-by-step processes for how to work. Jayne Groll, CEO of DevOps Institute, emphasized this point by saying, "There are no processes which are inherent to DevOps." In fact, many of the processes that DevOps practitioners rely on are based on ITIL. However, as you look to apply DevOps principles to how you work, you must look for opportunities to automate, empower, and focus on collaboration.

When looking at the processes related to DevSecOps, you must determine how to apply DevSecOps culture and principles to the processes of security management. Fundamentally, DevSecOps processes are:

- Lightweight
- Automated
- Trustful
- Measured
- Driving ownership and accountability
- Transparent
- Empowering
- Engendering of psychological safety
- Focused on developing a learning culture

If you integrate these principles into existing processes and find processes that enable them, you will build DevSecOps into everything you do.

UNDERSTANDING PROCESSES AT SCALE

When considering processes for an organization, the size and the maturity of an organization are key determinants. As organizations become larger, more advanced processes are needed to align the component parts. This, however, does not mean that processes need to be burdensome or slow things down. In fact, when an enterprise is moving faster, they need to have the process framework in place to ensure smooth and consistent execution. In a small company of only five or ten people, it is much easier for everyone to know what everyone else is doing at any given time. With smaller companies, there is less need to track everything in detail. As companies grow, it becomes imperative that they have the processes to track activities and react when problems arise.

When companies are performing tens or even hundreds of releases a day, they need to have a record of releases, so when something breaks, they can quickly find and easily understand what changed. For midsize to large companies, you need to know what is changing, what the process is, and who needs to get involved to engage the right people and respond quickly to get services restored during major incidents.

DevSecOps FOR IT SERVICE MANAGEMENT

IT Service Management (ITSM) is the set of processes a company uses to manage its technology products and services. The Information Technology Infrastructure Library (ITIL) is a framework for ITSM. ITIL provides process frameworks for the management of technology and alignment with the delivery of value to the customer. ITIL includes processes such as incident management, problem management, and change management. As mentioned in Chapter 1, "Introducing DevSecOps," there is a common misconception that DevOps and ITIL are fundamentally incompatible. This is actually far from reality. ITIL is a framework from which you can take or leave portions you like; it provides many useful processes for DevOps. As DevSecOps is based around a culture of collaboration, a process framework can integrate very well with a culture of collaboration.

Integrating process frameworks such as ITIL with DevSecOps principles becomes increasingly critical at scale:

- *Incident management* is a great example of the need for these processes. When you have millions of moving pieces and hundreds of globally distributed teams, it is significantly more important that you have a framework for responding appropriately when something goes wrong. At a small scale, everyone knows who wrote the code—it may even be the same engineer who set up the server on which the code runs, so diagnosing and responding have lower coordination requirements. At a large scale, you must have a process in place to coordinate and track across different systems, different teams, and different geographies.

- *Problem management* is another ITIL process that's critical to DevSecOps, as it focuses on understanding and remediating the root cause of incidents. This sort of review and evaluation is a key component of a learning culture. To be good at collaboration, DevSecOps engineers are also constantly looking at the underlying causes of incidents to learn from them and drive continuous improvement. The best DevSecOps teams are the ones that are not just reacting when an incident occurs, but being proactive and making sure they don't occur in the first place.

- *Change management* is another key ITIL process. When implemented poorly, it can be an impediment to rapid release cycles that serve as a cornerstone of great DevOps practices. However, by implementing change management with DevOps principles in mind, you can use the ITIL change management process to enable rapid releases, encourage DevOps practices, and improve stability.

One way to do this is by taking an adaptive approach to change management to balance risk with business agility. An adaptive approach can account for the level of automation and resilience built into the software and release process to allow for rapid releases while automatically tracking all changes to the system. This same adaptive approach can also ensure that higher-risk releases get the appropriate level of scrutiny and that dependencies across organizations are appropriately managed. In this way, a DevOps approach to the ITIL change management process can enhance collaboration and improve stability while enabling rapid release cycles.

SECURITY INCIDENT MANAGEMENT

The service management process of incident management is focused on the resolution of issues impacting technology services. Tightly honed incident management processes rely on collaboration between teams to drive the rapid resolution of issues and are therefore a good opportunity for the application of DevSecOps tools and principles. Tools such as enterprise chat and notification systems can help ensure that the right people are engaged at the right team, while practices such as blameless postmortems help ensure continuous improvement.

There is a lot of incident management activity that can happen before an incident occurs. From clear roles and responsibility to tightly honed instrumentation, DevSecOps principles can be applied to prevent incidents from happening in the first place and reduce their impact when they do occur.

DevSecOps focuses a lot on *system telemetry*, which is the data you collect about how your systems and services are performing, and for good reason. If you can instrument your systems properly, you can find issues before they impact customers and prevent minor incidents from becoming major incidents. In addition, if systems are properly instrumented, you can begin to apply machine learning and predictive analytics to anticipate incidents before they happen.

As mentioned previously, DevOps has its roots in Lean manufacturing, and many of the concepts of Lean are reflected in DevSecOps practices. One of the processes it borrows from Lean is the *Andon*

Cord. In Lean, the Andon Cord is a cord that shuts down an assembly line when something goes wrong. This decentralizes the decision to stop the assembly line and ensures that all resources are brought to bear on localized problems that impact the end-to-end delivery of a product. You can apply similar concepts to incident management by allowing anyone to declare an incident when there is a system error. In addition, you can bring all resources to bear on an issue with the concept of *swarming* to ensure that incidents are resolved as quickly as possible.

As discussed in Chapter 3, "DevSecOps People," a big part of the DevOps culture is accountability. In a trust-based culture, people working on incidents focus on resolving the issues rather than deferring blame or pointing fingers. This idea of accountability is aided by the concept of functional teams and full-stack engineers. Full-stack engineers focus on the system as a whole rather than individual vertical slices, while functional teams focus on isolated functionality, which can be developed without dependence on other teams. As a result of these structures, engineers can take full responsibility for resolving issues within their domains rather than needing to "throw them over the wall" to another team that might have shared responsibility. This practice is very much in line with proper incident management processes and ultimately leads to faster resolution times.

The ephemeral nature of systems in modern DevOps architectures has fundamentally changed the approach to incident management. For these applications and services, maintaining the state is no longer important, so incident responders can easily restart the systems on which applications run. In fact, in some cases, you can kill the whole application or service. For services with ephemeral infrastructure, the resolution process changes from investigate and diagnose to rapid restart and restore procedures, leading to significant improvements in resolution times. This is not to say that you should disregard diagnosis; it is important to capture important information such as application and system logs so that diagnosis can happen at a later time. Without further investigation or post-incident reviews, you cannot build a learning culture nor can you prevent repeat incidents from occurring. However, this approach allows you to separate restoration from investigation.

CHANGE MANAGEMENT

Change management is the IT service management process focusing on managing changes to the technical environment to ensure that the new changes are successfully made while minimizing negative impact. Change management can be particularly important for security, as appropriate change management can help ensure that changes adhere to an organization's security policies. Change management is another example of an ITIL-based process that can be significantly improved by the application of DevOps principles.

Change management is often implemented in ways that fly in the face of DevOps. Traditional implementations put multiple layers of approval in place for every change, inserting significant bureaucracy and gates that almost guarantee longer release cycles and delays in getting value to the customer. This fundamentally contradicts the DevOps emphasis of short release cycles and the rapid delivery of value to customers.

However, there can be little argument that tracking changes in a technical environment can be highly valuable. Especially in large environments, with small batch deployments, where many different changes are occurring at the same time, it is critical to have visibility into what is changing and how those changes might impact one another and, ultimately, the end customer. By bringing DevOps principles to bear on change management, you can ensure that you are tracking and managing changes while enabling speed and agility.

Instead of using change management as a gate to prevent change, use it as a process to enable change to get to your customers quickly and securely.

A DevOps approach to change management requires that you shift the focus of change management from the myopic focus on security and stability. You must broaden your perspective to understand change management as a process that enables security and agility while ensuring stability. Instead of using change management as a gate to prevent change, use it as a process to enable change to get to your customers quickly and securely.

Companies today are often doing tens and even hundreds of releases a day using continuous integration and continuous deployment. To do change management at this pace, you must automate your change management process. ITSM workflow tools such as Service Now expose *Application Programming Interfaces (APIs)*, which define and allow for other applications to interface with them on a programmatic basis. These APIs allow you to easily integrate your CD pipeline with your change management system. Using these APIs, you can automatically create change tickets. This ensures that there is a ticket for every change without causing additional burden or slowing down your deployment process.

Adaptive Change Management

If you take a DevOps approach to change management, you can implement adaptive change management. The goal of adaptive change management is to implement lightweight, scalable, and agile processes to improve stability while enabling delivery velocity. This process takes into account the risk of a change, thereby ensuring that the appropriate amount of attention is paid to high-risk changes without slowing down low-risk changes. This approach also provides a mechanism for teams to lower their risk, thus driving down friction and encouraging continuous improvement.

In this approach to change management, every change is assigned a risk based on a risk calculation by the team implementing the change. This aligns with the overarching goal of ensuring that you are appropriately managing risk and adapting to it. Approval and oversight levels are then dynamically adjusted based on the risk of a given change. In addition, release times can be adjusted in accordance with risk levels.

Approaches such as continuous integration and continuous deployment (CI/CD) and deploying updates to a small subset of users, referred to as *A/B deployments*, lower the risk level of a given change. With adaptive change management, low-risk changes—with fully automated testing using CI/CD and A/B deployments—are released without any approvals. On the other hand, high-risk changes, which may require coordination with multiple teams and may be highly manual, receive review from all teams that may be impacted. This ensures collaboration and appropriate integration testing at all levels.

Change Risk Calculation

Risk calculation for a change can be aligned with standard methods of using the impact and probability of a risk. In this approach, probability reflects the likelihood that a given risk will occur, while impact reflects the impact on the business if a risk occurs regardless of the probability. That is, assuming the change fails, what is the level of impact on the business? It is important that teams be allowed to assess their own impact and risk. Allowing teams to assess their own risk aligns with the DevOps concepts of accountability and trust. By trusting teams to accurately assess the risk of a change, you can build a high-trust culture that drives high-performance companies.

> *Some may balk at the idea of self-assessment, decrying that they cannot trust the releasors to accurately assess the risk of their changes favoring rapid delivery over stability. However, the reality is that this is not the case for high-trust environments, where development and operations teams alike are focused on the success of the customer. That said, you can put mitigating controls in place if needed. One way to do this is to weigh the risk rating based on a team's past performance as well as their ability to accurately rate the risk of a change. For example, if you are rating risk using high-, medium-, and low-risk ratings, a team with a failed change in the past 10 releases might increase from a low-risk rating to a medium. This risk weighting would then be removed once the team had reestablished a history of successful releases. By bringing actual performance back into the risk rating, you can build a numerical feedback format and allay concerns that some may game the system.*

Guiding Principles for Change Review and Approval

Once the risk of a change is calculated, the review and approvals can be adjusted to align with the level of risk of a given change. Low-risk changes may require review from managers. Higher-risk changes may require coordination with other teams when there are cross-dependencies and, in such situations, may benefit from review by a change advisory board (CAB). When aligning approvals with risk, keep in mind these guiding principles:

- The closer the change reviewer is to the technical details of the code, the better. That is, an engineer on the same development team will have a much better idea of the impact of a code change than the vice president of that group.

- While high trust is critical, an audit should require that there be another set of eyes reviewing changes to prevent people from making illicit or damaging changes when they have malicious intent.

- The CAB, if one is needed, should act as a "flight control," coordinating between different teams and business needs. The CAB should not be a bureaucratic body designed to stop changes.

- Small, incremental changes are safer. Instead of making major updates, strive to continually improve small portions of the application or service.

- The easier you can make it to submit a change, the more likely people are to follow the process.

With these principles in mind, you can develop an approval system that ensures proper oversight while allowing changes to production to be as frictionless as possible.

Standard Changes and "Change Freezes"

In addition to these types of changes, there are also standard changes that do not require approval. This is the ideal state for changes in a DevSecOps world, where small changes can be released almost continuously to production.

Standard changes are pre-approved changes that are extremely low risk, relatively common, and follow a set process. This is an idea for changes that can be deployed in a fully automated manner using

CI/CD, which includes best practices such as continuous testing, automated rollback, feature flags, and the like. These sorts of changes can be approved to be standard changes. For a change to qualify as a standard change, it must be low risk and have a history of successful performance. Once approved, these standard changes can be deployed without any approval other than the code review. This is ideal for an organization that wants to move quickly. By encouraging as many changes as possible to go through the standard change process, organizations can reduce organizational bureaucracy and increase time to market.

It is important to note that timing can play an important part in change management, as it can impact the risk of a change. Periods of high activity, such as Cyber Monday for commerce platforms as well as major company events, can be high-risk times for a business. Often it is desirable to do whatever is possible during these times to minimize risk.

The evidence indicates that "change freezes" simply do not work.

Change freezes are a common practice among many business where, during critical business periods, no changes are allowed. However, the evidence indicates that change freezes simply do not work. There are multiple reasons these do not work, the first of which is that they are hardly, if ever, actually adhered to. The fact is that, even during high-risk times, business and technology must continue to move forward. Whether it is an emergency fix for a customer issue or business critical release, there are almost always exceptions to change freezes. This happens so much so that change freezes are often referred to as *change slushes*.

Data shows that change freezes often cause a huge influx of changes directly before the freeze, where teams try to cram in all their critical features directly before a high risk, leading to significant instability during the very period of time that the business is trying to protect. In addition, there is a flood of releases directly after the change freeze period, which shows that a backlog of changes has built up and the company is losing out on delivering value to the customer during that period. Figure 4.1 shows change data from a major media company that depicts exactly this scenario.

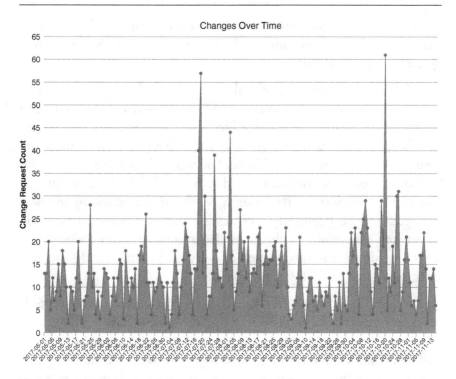

Figure 4.1 The rate of change shows a significant spike in the number of releases directly before and after a "change freeze" period.

Can you guess where the change freeze was? Not only is there a massive spike in the number of releases before and after the change freeze period, but the number of changes during the period shows only a slight decrease.

The final problem with change freeze periods is that they treat low-risk changes the same way they treat high-risk changes—with a blanket statement that "Thou shalt not change." One way to address these issues is to simply approach it for what it is: a high-risk period. With that in mind, you can simply raise the risk of any changes during that period. Starting from an adaptive approach to change management, you can raise the risk of all change so that low-risk changes are evaluated as medium risk changes, medium as high, and high as critical. (Note that this necessitates the creation of an additional level of risk, which is higher than high.) This does a good job of accurately reflecting the business reality without imposing a somewhat arbitrary, unrealistic blanket statement, which is rarely enforced. The reality is that this is a higher risk time for the business, and any changes should be evaluated with this in mind.

Of course, testing is a critical success factor for any change management process to be successful. All testing—from the unit level to integration testing to vulnerability testing—is important. The key here is to automate wherever possible and to build this automation into your deployment pipeline. Additional details on building a DevSecOps deployment pipeline with automated security validation are available in Chapter 5, "DevSecOps Technology," With automated testing in place, resources can be deployed to do testing that is more exploratory in nature and that might catch things that automated testing would not. This test automation can be used in every environment and should be integrated into the deployment pipeline.

There is a balance here from a time perspective in that these tests must test full system functionality but also cannot take much time if they are going to be used in a rapidly deploying pipeline. This balance will vary from team to team, but it must not be so time-consuming that teams are tempted to skip testing or to do less frequent releases. Ultimately, it is the responsibility of the team developing the code to determine this balance. They must ensure that code is delivered to customers without issues. Once testing is automated and proven successful, it is easy to advocate that these changes be included as standard changes, enabling rapid and seamless delivery to the customers.

In all this planning and risk classification, it is important to remember that there will always be unplanned/emergency changes and you must ensure that your process accounts for these. To maintain the adaptability of your change management process even under emergency circumstances, you can continue to use the classification and approval matrices described in this chapter. However, in emergency circumstances, modifications must be made so that changes can be made even quicker. To accommodate rapid change, it is often important to allow verbal approval for these sorts of changes. It is often also appropriate to delay the filing of any change forms until after the emergency situation has been remediated. By making these adjustments, you can ensure that a process that is already designed for rapid deployment can become even faster to handle emergencies without sacrificing the necessary review and oversight.

Problem Management

Problem management is another critical ITIL process for security professionals and one that closely aligns with DevOps principles. Problem management looks at, and attempts to address, the underlying causes of incidents. In doing so, you have an opportunity to help build the learning culture critical to DevSecOps. By looking to mitigate the underlying causes of incidents, problem management also builds into the culture a process that drives continual improvement, another key element of DevSecOps.

According to the IT Process Wiki, "The primary objectives of this ITIL process are to prevent incidents from happening, and to minimize the impact of incidents that cannot be prevented."[1] To do this, problem management looks at the root causes for incidents and determines actions to be taken. Taking a DevSecOps approach here means that the focus must be on continuous learning rather than blame or corrective action.

Problem Management at Wiley

Wiley takes problem management seriously, making a dedicated effort to identify and reduce problems. At Wiley I introduced an availability manager whose sole focus is managing the availability and performance of its products and services for researchers and learners around the world.

The Wiley incident managers perform a dual role of incident manager and problem manager so that the people responsible for resolving the incident can also take actions to help ensure they do not occur in the future. The availability

(continues)

---

[1] Kempter, Stefan. "Problem Management." IT Process Wiki. IT Process Maps, March 10, 2022. https://wiki.en.it-processmaps.com/index.php/Problem_Management.

(*continued*)

manager, in conjunction with the incident/problem managers, launched a focused effort to identify and reduce incidents. This focus effort enabled Wiley to close almost 200 outstanding problems. By reducing the underlying causes of incidents, Wiley was able to reduce the number and severity of incidents. During that same time period, availability across all applications rose by .64 percent. While that may seem like a small number, when we are talking about availability and getting to multiple nines, this represents a huge improvement for the customers.

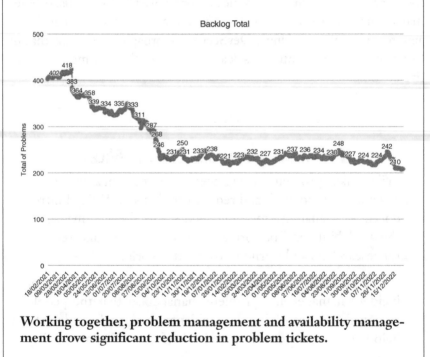

Working together, problem management and availability management drove significant reduction in problem tickets.

The first step in the problem management process is the identification of the problem. This can be done by examining incident trends to determine what common underlying causes may be. Many organizations follow the problem management process for all major incidents (generally defined as P1 or P2 incidents) to ensure that every major incident has follow-up to drive continuous improvement. It is, however, important to stress that problem management should not be reserved only for major incidents. Often it is the minor incidents that are most insidious. There is the risk of "death by 1,000 paper cuts," that is, many small issues can be as bad as, if not worse than, one major one. Problem managers and availability managers should be looking for trends and repeat incidents and trends to be included as part of the problem management process.

While this approach may incur the additional cost of availability managers, this cost outweighs the detrimental impact of outages and performance degradation. The cost to brand reputation for numerous small issues can be just as serious as major outages. In addition, by proactively addressing the root cause of incidents, you can significantly reduce the amount of valuable time your engineers focus on firefighting.

The *incident postmortem*, also referred to as the *post-incident review* (PIR), is the first step in problem management and an excellent opportunity to instill institutional learning for an organization. During this process, the underlying cause may be determined or a temporary fix applied. If the underlying root cause is known, the problem can be classified as a *known error* until the underlying cause(s) are resolved. If the underlying cause cannot be determined, then actions can be taken to improve handling and preparations or work-arounds before it occurs again.

> *Problem management requires focused work and dedication. Problem management does not "just happen" because postmortems are happening. For midsize to large companies, resources need to be assigned to problem management.*

The Problem Manager Role

In more and more companies, incident managers are playing dual roles as incident and problem managers. This can be a useful model, as the incident managers are often the closest to the incidents; however, this combination of roles cannot happen at the expense of problem resolution. If incident managers are too busy firefighting to take time to build a better fire engine, then improvement will not be made, and the team will be mired in daily toil. For the combined role of incident manager and problem manager to work, it is often necessary to have someone whose job it is to identify and drive the resolution of problems. This is one of the most rewarding processes, as resolving the causes of incidents and improving daily work are key elements to DevSecOps. There are cost and flow efficiencies here. The combined role also reduces hand-offs and thereby increases efficiency. If you can do problem management well, it reduces toil in day-to-day work by reducing the amount of effort spent on a daily basis fighting fires.

If incident managers are too busy firefighting to take time to build a better fire engine, then improvement will not be made, and the team will be mired in daily toil.

Blameless Postmortems

Learning culture is a key component of DevSecOps, and this type of learning can be instilled in organizations through the ITIL process of incident postmortems. This DevSecOps principle is highlighted in Gene Kim's Third Way of DevOps: "creating a culture that fosters two things: continual experimentation, taking risks and learning from failure."

It is important that postmortems be approached with a spirit of learning rather than a spirit of blame. To build a culture of continual learning, all resources involved in the incident use the incident postmortem as an opportunity for the organization to grow and learn.

A good postmortem creates an environment of psychological safety where the team can feel free to explore the issue. In blameless postmortems, the engineers walk through the incident detailing each event as it happened from their perspective. Engineers who were involved in the incident detail their observations, expectations, and the timeline of events. The key goal of such a postmortem is not just to solve the "problem," or to find the "root cause," but also to ensure that organizational learning occurs. At the end of a postmortem, one of the key items that everyone involved must ask themselves is "What did I learn?" If everyone leaving the postmortem has learned something, then the postmortem should be considered a success even if no further action is taken.

If everyone leaving the postmortem has learned something, then the postmortem should be considered a success even if no further action is taken.

It is critical that postmortems not focus on finding a single root cause or finding someone to blame. In *The Unicorn Project*, as they are beginning their postmortem meeting, Kurt (a key QA manager helping to lead change at Parts Unlimited) notes this stating, "The spirit and intent of these sessions are to learn from them, chronicling what happened before memories fade. Prevention requires honesty, and honesty requires the absence of fear."[2]

As mentioned, blame-based cultures discourage the experimentation and learning required to be successful in today's marketplace. Looking for blame will only ensure that the full story is not revealed because people do not feel comfortable sharing what happens. In Etsy's famous Code as Craft blog post, "Blameless PostMortems and a Just Culture," John Allspaw writes, "A funny thing happens when engineers make mistakes and feel safe when giving details about it: they are not only willing to be held accountable, they are also enthusiastic in helping the rest of the company avoid the same error in the future."[3] Postmortems provide an excellent opportunity to show engineers how they can be rewarded for their honesty. By providing space for open and honest discussion, leaders can play a big part in building a learning culture.

RELEASE MANAGEMENT

Release management is an ITIL process that fundamentally changes with the technology of DevSecOps. No longer does release management need to be a set of manual steps executed by different people, each taking separate actions to ensure the successful release of a new product. Deployment tools such as Jenkins enable CI/CD in a fully automated manner. CI/CD is a cornerstone of DevOps and DevSecOps, as it enables the small incremental releases that are at the core of DevOps. CI/CD enables core principles of DevOps such as flow, fast feedback, experimentation, and continuous learning.

---

[2] Kim, Gene. 2019. The Unicorn Project: A Novel About Developers, Digital Disruption, and Thriving in the Age of Data. 1st ed. Portland: IT Revolution Press.

[3] "Blameless PostMortems and a Just Culture." Code as Craft. Etsy, May 22, 2012. www.etsy.com/codeascraft/blameless-postmortems.

In addition, these mechanisms that allow for the rapid deployment of software and infrastructure can also be leveraged to enable automated testing and automated security scanning. By interjecting security tooling into the deployment pipeline, you can ensure that all releases meet the security standards of your organization. Because deployment pipelines can be leveraged to deploy infrastructure as code (IaC), you can employ security scanning in your deployment pipelines to ensure that the software and hardware meet your security standards. In addition, these pipelines can be used to automate compliance, alleviating the need for manual testing and evidence collection.

Chapter 5 provides details about DevSecOps pipelines and how to integrate security into the deployment process. From a process perspective, what is important to note is that, through automation, you can eliminate the laborious manual release processes of yesterday by automating deployment from start to finish with CI/CD.

A DevOps Approach to Security Processes

Many of the standard security processes and practices also enable a DevSecOps culture when they are done right. Practices such as tabletop exercises and red team/blue team exercises help build a culture of collaboration and continuous learning that's critical to DevSecOps. These processes have been part of cybersecurity for quite some time, so the key is to ensure they are approached with the principles of DevOps, encouraging learning culture, collaboration, and trust.

Tabletop Exercises

Tabletop exercises for cybersecurity allow cross-functional teams to virtually simulate cyber-attacks and the responses. In tabletop exercises, a specified attack is described, and then, in a serial fashion, participants discuss their actions in the process to identify and remediate the situation. Tabletop exercises provide a great way to ensure appropriate response in a low-risk environment. These exercises help build awareness across the organization, help clarify roles and responsibilities as well as key decision-making capabilities, and help identify potential gaps in the process.

Tabletops exercises offer many benefits, including the following:

- Increased awareness of threats across teams within a business
- Opportunities to evaluate incident preparedness
- Determination of gaps in the incident response process
- Clarification of roles and responsibilities as well as decision-making
- Identification of potential capability gaps

Tabletop exercises become increasingly valuable for addressing wide-reaching scenarios, such as ransomware attacks, which may require participation from many departments including legal, finance, marketing, development, and operations. For critical situations, tabletop exercises can be a great way to raise awareness and build collaboration between the teams, again stressing that security is not the job of any one team, but a way that all teams become involved.

Attack Simulation: Red Team, Blue Team, Purple Team

Similar to tabletop exercises, *attack simulations* offer an opportunity to embed cybersecurity learning into the culture. Red team/blue team exercises are attack simulations in which one group of people is designated the red team with the goal of breaching the security. Another group, designated the blue team, is charged with defending against the attack. To protect against unintended consequences to production systems, these simulations are often performed in preproduction or isolated accounts with copies of production systems. These exercises are similar to tabletop exercises, in that they test the defenses through simulated attacks. However, in these exercises, the teams are working hands on with the systems they are trying to protect.

These types of exercise are critical to DevSecOps because they help establish a learning culture by actively involving all teams to think about creative ways to attack and defend their systems. To build this culture across the organization, it is important to include people outside of the security organization—such as development, operations, and platform engineering—in these drills. These exercises often include a purple team, whose responsibility it is to help coordinate and monitor the simulation. The purple team can further facilitate learning though careful observation and data analysis, identify potential gaps, and make suggestions for future improvements.

As with tabletop exercises, it is important to make this a regular and repeated process. It is not enough to do this once. To build these tests into the culture, it is best to find a regular cadence where these sorts of events are repeated, potentially on different systems, potentially with different participants. Whether that be quarterly, semi-annually, or even annually, the key is to ensure it is planned on a regular cadence to truly build it into the culture.

CHAOS ENGINEERING

Chaos engineering is a great DevOps practice that can be adapted to DevSecOps. Chaos engineering helps build system resilience by intentionally interjecting errors, such as server shutdowns, latency increases, and resource exhaustion, into a system. The concept of chaos engineering originated at Netflix in 2011 and was designed to help ensure stability in Netflix's cloud platform. Casey Rosenthal, who built the Chaos Engineering team at Netflix, defines chaos engineering as "the discipline of experimenting on a distributed system in order to build confidence in the system's capability to withstand turbulent conditions in production."[4]

To implement chaos testing, Netflix developed the widely known Chaos Monkey to inject random errors. The initial system randomly brought down systems (EC2 instances) within Amazon Web Services (AWS) to ensure the system was resilient to these types of failures. Chaos Monkey was later expanded into a set of tools known as the Simian Army. Chaos Monkey and the tools within the Simian Army are open-source and available for download on GitHub.

---

[4] Rosenthal, Casey. "What Chaos Engineering Is (and Isn'T)." DevOps.Com. June 25, 2021. https://devops.com/what-chaos-engineering-is-and-isnt.

With any highly complex system, failure is inevitable, so you need to prepare for failure rather than just try to prevent it.

Chaos engineering speaks to a larger mental shift from assuming that, if designed correctly, systems would behave correctly to assuming that systems will fail and building them to be resilient to that type of failure. One of the reasons this type of testing is important is because of the increasing complexity of our systems.

Previous state-based systems assumed that servers in the data center would not go down and therefore could safely store the state of the application locally. Modern design acknowledges that this is not a safe assumption. Not only will systems occasionally fail, but as systems become increasingly complex, more components mean more opportunities for failure.

With any system of sufficient complexity, full knowledge of the system is ultimately not possible. It is, therefore, not possible to fully test a system based on knowledge of that system. Engineers must design systems to expect failure and be resilient to that failure from the ground up. In the same way, you must design for security attacks and breaches from the ground up. It is important to keep in mind that, with any highly complex system, failure is inevitable, so you need to prepare for failure rather than just try to prevent it.

Chaos testing is also important because it allows you to learn while not in the middle of an incident. By intentionally injecting failure conditions, you can observe how the system reacts when you're not in the middle of a firefight. While incidents offer great learning opportunities, they are rarely an ideal time to learn because the people involved in resolving the incident are under pressure and laser focused on getting things back in working order.

Testing of this nature not only tests the systems for resilience but also tests the systems around these systems—such as people, processes, and monitoring. With testing of this type, you see not only that the system is resilient but also how monitoring and instrumentation behaves as well as any people involved in the management of these systems.

Chaos testing can be quite successful for cybersecurity. The testers should begin with a hypothesis and then develop an automated way of testing that hypothesis. In this way, known error conditions can be tested. For example, test the hypothesis that, if a container with a known vulnerability were created in production, the Security Operations team would be notified.

With that hypothesis in mind, you can design a test to insert cybersecurity error conditions and observe the results. Other failure scenarios might include catching AWS instances deployed with default permissions, or introducing code or infrastructure with critical vulnerabilities that should be caught and/or blocked. If you can design tests of this nature in an automated way, it will help ensure that the tools that you think are protecting you are working correctly, not only during normal operating conditions but also when error conditions arise.

CONCLUSION

The processes of DevSecOps come from many sources: they come from ITIL, they come from security, they come from quality assurance. What is important about these processes—what they have in common and what makes them DevSecOps processes—is that they apply the DevOps principles and leverage automation to reduce human toil. By taking a lightweight and automated approach to traditional processes, you can reduce steps in processes and even make these processes completely transparent to engineers without eliminating the value these processes were created to deliver. By applying DevOps principles, you take traditional processes and use them to empower engineers and build the learning culture that is critical to successful DevSecOps implementation.

CHAPTER 5

DevSecOps Technology

INTRODUCTION

DevSecOps technology enables and underpins the core principles of DevOps, but it is important to reiterate that DevSecOps and DevOps are not just about technology. DevSecOps is primarily about culture and the DevOps principles. With this in mind, it is important to clarify just what constitutes a DevSecOps tool. What defines DevSecOps technology? The reality is that there is no such thing as a "DevSecOps" tool, but, rather, a set of tools that enable DevSecOps. While this may seem like a subtle differentiation, it is an important one because how a tool is used impacts the outcome. If you think of DevSecOps as a culture of collaboration, then you can consider a set of tools that enable collaboration. More generally, you can think of DevSecOps tools as the set of security tools that enables the core principles of DevOps.

The reality is, there is no such thing as a "DevSecOps" tool, but, rather, a set of tools that enable DevSecOps. . . . If you think of DevSecOps as a culture of collaboration, then you can consider a set of tools that enables collaboration.

Marketing messages make this point more confusing, as many modern security tools now purport to be a "DevSecOps tool." It is important to consider what a DevSecOps tool actually is to separate reality from the marketing messages. Tools like *extended detection and response (XDR)*, which monitor the environment, focus on core principles such as observability and transparency. However, if these tools are not shared with others who are responsible for these systems, they can actually be contradictory to DevOps principles. Tools are, ultimately, just a means to an end and can be used in many different ways. So, when understanding if something is a "DevSecOps tool," you must look at tools that enable the core principles of DevOps. You must understand how to use technology to enable collaboration, rapid feedback, continuous learning, and small batch delivery.

You must look for tools that enable DevSecOps principles such as these:

- **Collaboration**—As collaboration is at the core of DevSecOps, you must look for tools that enable better collaboration across teams. Chat tools such as Slack or Teams promote the free flow of information required for collaboration in global hybrid team environments. In addition, tools such as PagerDuty can help coordinate and communicate between teams when issues arise.

- **Flow of value from left to right**—CI/CD tools such as Jenkins and CircleCI are the key to Gene Kim's First Way of DevOps, allowing for the smooth and continuous flow of value to the customer. In addition, automation in its many forms helps eliminate daily toil, thereby allowing engineers to focus on building great products and services for the customers. This automation can take the form of security orchestration, automation, and response (SOAR) tools or custom scripts. As long as the focus is on reducing manual work, they help support flow of value to the customers.

- **Empowerment**—By giving engineers more control over the application life cycle from development to production support, you empower them, which drives better business results. Abstraction layers such as cloud providers and automated security testing allow engineers to do the right thing without requiring hand-offs or dependence on other teams.

- **Fast feedback and continuous learning**—Small batch delivery enabled by CI/CD tools enables rapid feedback from the customers, thus allowing engineers to rapidly see the impact their changes are having for their customers. In addition, shared telemetry from monitoring and observability tools can provide critical visibility to the impact of changes.

- **Shift Left**—Using test-driven development and inserting security testing in the pipeline can increase the quality of your service and give you more confidence to release faster and more frequently.

THE FALLACY OF A "DevSecOps TOOL"

No tool is inherently a "DevSecOps tool." This is because alignment with DevOps principles is dependent on how a tool is used. I have seen tools designed for, and marketed as, DevSecOps used in ways that are fundamentally at odds with the core DevOps principles.

During my time running a global DevOps consulting firm, we worked with one team that had three different chat platforms. The development team used Slack, the security team used Teams, and the business teams used HipChat. This use of these tools actually reenforced silos and discouraged communication between the teams. In this way, chat tools, arguably one of the tools that can clearly enhance collaboration, was being used in a way that actually prevented collaboration across teams. When considering what a "DevSecOps tool" is, it is important to look not just at the tool's function, but also at how it is being used.

DevSecOps CONTINUOUS INTEGRATION AND CONTINUOUS DEPLOYMENT

Continuous integration and continuous deployment (CI/CD) is a cornerstone of DevOps principles and practices, as it enables small batch delivery by providing short feedback loops and strengthening input from the customer. The CI/CD process includes all the steps to take changes to code from the developer and get them built and deployed to the customer. This includes the following steps:

1. Pushing the code from the source code repository
2. Integrating it into the rest of the application

3. Building a complete application

4. Testing the application

5. Deploying the application to production all through automation

This is in stark contrast to older methods, where developers would manually build their code in isolation and then send it to testers to examine, who would log and report any errors they encountered.

CI/CD is the process for rapid building and deploying of applications. Continuous integration allows developers to integrate their code with the code of other developers who are working on the same application or service at any time. Continuous deployment takes this code and builds it into a deployable state so that it can be pushed to production at any time. It should be noted that continuous deployment does not mean that applications are always deployed to the customer, only that the application is always in a deployable state. While delivering the product to customers quickly is important, constant changes to the application may cause a suboptimal experience for the end users. Timing is crucial in determining when certain changes are launched. Therefore, continuous deployment pipelines may simply build the production-ready package to be available for deployment when scheduled or may deploy every change depending on the business requirements.

CI/CD provides amazing improvements in direct feedback to the developers. By getting small incremental changes to customers quickly, engineers get rapid feedback on the impact their changes are having for their customers. The deployment pipeline also provides tremendous opportunities for security. By incorporating security tools in the deployment process, you can ensure that code is secure before it ever gets to a production environment.

Figure 5.1 shows a basic CI/CD diagram. At each stage of the deployment pipeline, different tools can be used to ensure the security of the release. These tools, as well as a selection of the top vendors in each area, are listed. While this is not a comprehensive picture of all available tools or providers, it should provide some idea about the variety of vendors available to you as you build out your pipeline. Note that some tools are available in multiple stages because they can be used at multiple points throughout the CI/CD pipeline. The following sections go into more detail about the stages of the deployment pipeline and the tools that can be used at each stage.

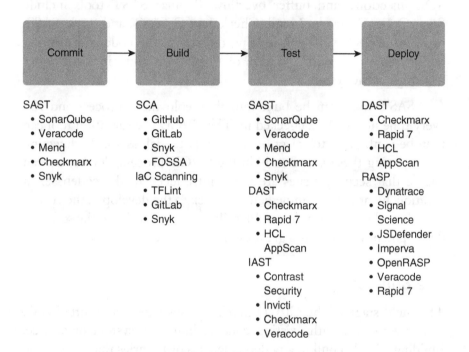

Figure 5.1 The DevSecOps pipeline integrates security tools directly into the process of building and deploying applications and services.

The Commit Stage

Commit is generally the first step in the DevOps CI/CD pipeline. Developers commit their code to a source code repository to provide a centralized source for storing code and tracking versioning accurately. To appropriately manage the code, all source code should be checked into a shared repository. There are many source code repositories including GitHub, Bitbucket, SourceForge, and GitLab. Cloud providers have their own source code repositories, such as AWS CodeCommit and Azure Repos.

The commit stage is a great early opportunity to verify the security of the code. Static code analysis tools such as static application security testing (SAST) can insert security at the first step in the CI/CD pipeline. SAST can analyze the code committed to determine if there are any potential security weaknesses, such as cross-site scripting, SQL injections, and buffer overflow. Popular SAST tools include SonarQube, Veracode, Mend, Checkmarx CxSAST, and Snyk. SAST provides *white-box analysis,* looking directly at the code and offering considerable protection because of the full visibility into the inner workings of the system.

SAST tools can be built into the deployment process and run every time new code is checked in. The CI/CD orchestration tool can then be configured to reject or flag any potential issues. By detecting and rejecting these issues early in the CI/CD process, developers can ensure that security issues are never introduced to the codebase. In addition, by providing immediate feedback to the developer, the cost to remediate these issues is lower. Identifying issues earlier in the software development life cycle is a great example of the concept of Shift Left.

The Build Stage

The build stage of the CI/CD pipeline takes newly committed code and integrates it with existing code to build the system or service. Building will also pull in any dependencies or libraries that need to be included in the final product. The build stage usually produces a completed package that is ready to be tested and deployed.

A standard build process may include the following steps:

1. Compilation of all code that must be built to develop executable programs

2. *Linting,* which checks the code for programmatic and stylistic errors

3. Artifact generation, where the final package is prepared for deployment to production[1]

---

[1] Fernandez, Tomas. "Design an Effective Build Stage for Continuous Integration." Semaphore. December 7, 2022. https://semaphoreci.com/blog/build-stage.

The build phase should be used to incorporate any security standard tools and libraries. During the build phase, you can incorporate code for endpoint protection, dynamic application testing, and logging and tagging standards. You should use this opportunity to ensure that all your standard security tools are built into the product. This should include installation of endpoint detection and response (EDR) tools as well as dynamic application security testing (DAST) tools. Although these are runtime tools, you can use the build phase to ensure they are built into your solution. This is also a good time to verify that the tagging standards for your organization are adhered to, both for the application and for infrastructure deployments.

During the build phase, you can also use source composition analysis (SCA) to check for vulnerabilities in any dependencies or libraries. Third-party vulnerabilities are increasingly becoming a major area of risk for companies, as seen in the Apache Log4J breach. SCA looks at all source code to determine potential known vulnerabilities in linked libraries and open-source code references. SCA can also be used to identify any potential license violations that could cost companies a significant amount of money. Top SCA tools include GitHub, GitLab, Snyk, and FOSSA. By scanning at the build phase, you can ensure that the code that's submitted is secure and that external dependencies, such as open-source libraries, are secure as well.

The build phase is also a good point to scan any IaC for vulnerabilities related to components of your infrastructure. IaC scanning works in a similar manner to SAST tools, except that they focus on infrastructure-related vulnerabilities. Key tools in this category include TFLint, GitLab, and Snyk. By leveraging IaC scanning, you can ensure that your application and your infrastructure is secure.

The Test Stage

Once the build process is complete, automated testing of the compiled system can begin. The key for DevSecOps practices is to make security testing part of the process. This testing will be *black-box testing*, looking for ways to compromise the build system as a compiled whole. DAST can be deployed at this stage. DAST provides an outside-in evaluation of the applications and services. It helps identify vulnerabilities by simulating attacks in a way similar to how an external party would try to breach the application or service.

DAST tools are run against the compiled product. As part of the deployment process the application or service should be deployed to a staging environment where this sort of testing can be run. DAST tools search for vulnerabilities in a running application, such as cross-site scripting, external XML entities (XXE), cross-site request forgery (CSRF), or SQL injections that your SAST tool may not have caught. While static code analysis may identify some of these issues, it is important to run these tests against a running application. Because DAST tools are designed to be run against a dynamic environment, they can identify issues that your SAST tool may not.[2] It should be noted that while DAST tools are quite useful in identifying potential issues, they are inherently noisy and tend to produce a lot of false positives.

The Microfocus blog says "a DAST scanner can be thought of like a security guard. However, rather than just making sure the doors and windows are locked, this guard goes a step further by attempting to physically break into the building. The guard might try to pick the locks on the doors or break windows. After finishing this examination, the guard could report back to the building manager and provide an explanation of how he was able to break into the building." To extend this metaphor, SAST examines all the components of the lock to ensure the integrity of each one. DAST attempts to pick the fully assembled lock and your CI/CD pipeline coordinates all phases of the process, assembles and installs the lock, and coordinates the testing.

Interactive application security testing (IAST) provides another useful tool during the testing phase. IAST solutions instrument applications by deploying agents and sensors in running applications to analyze how the application performs during runtime, which can be simulated by testing. Unlike SAST and DAST, IAST is integrated into your codebase and runs when your code runs. It should be noted that because IAST runs only when your code runs, it will not test all code

---

[2] "What Is Dynamic Application Security Testing (DAST)?" OpenText. March 1, 2023. www.microfocus.com/en-us/what-is/dast.

but only those code paths that are executed during runtime. IAST provides instrumentation of the application code designed to identify and alert potential attacks and provides a useful tool in detecting security issues during functional and performance testing.

The Deploy Stage

The deployment phase makes the code available to users of the application or service. This is the point at which you transition from looking at the build time security vulnerabilities to identifying runtime vulnerabilities. Once an application or service has been pushed to production, the feature is available but so are any vulnerabilities or security flaws that still exist, which is why it is so critical to find and address any issues prior to this stage. In addition, new vulnerabilities may be discovered in already deployed code, so it is important to continuously scan the production environment for vulnerability.

The deployment stage also represents the point at which security logging, telemetry, and IAST happen. This is the point at which you can begin to see how the application performs under real-world scenarios and, at times, real-world attack scenarios. IAST runs in real time during application execution. In addition, runtime application self-protection (RASP) can detect intrusion attempts and respond to remediate those threats. Real-time logging and monitoring provide valuable insights into how the system is operating in production, thus helping to alert you to intrusion attempts and other malicious activities.

IDE Integration

Many companies are now integrating security testing directly into the tools that developers are using to develop their code, their integrated development environment (IDE). This extends the Shift Left paradigm, moving the security testing earlier in the development process and providing faster feedback to the developer. By implementing security testing directly into the IDE, developers do not need to wait to commit their code before they receive feedback.

The IDE is a great place to do static code analysis and check dependencies such as libraries using SAST and SCA. Tools such as Snyk and Contrast now offer the ability to integrate directly into the IDE, providing immediate feedback as the developer is working. This is akin to a word processor that highlights misspelled words as opposed to submitting a completed paper to someone else and then waiting for them to edit and return a marked-up version. Clearly, by providing direct and immediate feedback, the author of the code is empowered to take security concerns into their own hands without reliance on others, thus reducing the need for unnecessary handoffs.

While integration of security tools into the IDE provides a significant opportunity to shorten feedback loops, it will not provide testing of the fully built application nor will it catch runtime dependencies or even issues that occur when code is integrated with other code components. Therefore, it should not be seen as a substitute for IAST or DAST.

INFRASTRUCTURE AS CODE

IaC is another DevOps-related technology with significant opportunities for cybersecurity. IaC allows developers to describe the systems on which an application will run using code enabling the automated deployment not just of the application, but also the infrastructure on which it runs. Tools such as Terraform, CloudFormation, and Azure Resource Manager (ARM) allow engineers to describe the exact infrastructure as code.

IaC makes it easy to ensure consistency between development, testing, and production environments. It also provides the ability to easily re-create the entire environment from the ground up in disaster recovery scenarios. Because the code is checked in and managed by a source code repository, it also allows for changes to be easily rolled back if they are problematic. IaC ensures consistency, repeatability, traceability, and resilience.

The following Terraform code from HashiCorp's tutorial provides a basic example of code used to describe and deploy infrastructure:

```
terraform {
   required_providers {
      aws = {
      source  = "hashicorp/aws"
      version = "~> 4.16"
   }
 }
   required_version = ">= 1.2.0"
}

   provider "aws" {

 region  = "us-west-2"

}
resource "aws_instance" "app_server" {

ami            = "ami-830c94e3"

instance_type = "t2.micro"
tags = {
      Name = "ExampleAppServerInstance"
 }
}
```[3]

This code will automatically create a new server instance in the AWS US West region. This code is used to specify where the server will be deployed, what type of system it will be (t2.micro), and the name of the system (ExampleAppServerInstance).

While this simple example configures only a single application server, languages such as Terraform are immensely powerful and can be used to deploy highly complex environments.

Once this is executed, the infrastructure will be available for deploying the application. Additional tools such as Ansible can then be

---

[3] "Build Infrastructure." HashiCorp. Accessed April 18, 2023. https://learn.hashicorp.com/tutorials/terraform/aws-build.

used to deploy detailed system configuration. IaC can be integrated into the CI/CD pipeline so that it not only deploys the latest version of the code but also deploys the infrastructure as well as deploying everything needed for a fully functional system.

As with other Shift Left practices, IaC poses risks and opportunities. As IaC relies on templates for the deployment of infrastructure, an insecure template can easily replicate vulnerabilities across many environments. By the same light, that the template conforms to security standards, those standards will be present in all infrastructure that leverage those templates.

You can also use some of the same tools discussed for application security within your deployment pipeline to verify the security and compliance for infrastructure as code. SAST tools such as XenonStack and Snyk provide code analysis tools for your IaC code. And, because you are talking about code, you can build these checks into your deployment pipeline to ensure that it is secure.

One of the other security benefits that IaC offers is traceability. Because your infrastructure is code, you can treat it as such by checking it into a code repository and submitting any changes. Rather than allowing engineers to make changes directly via your cloud provider or hardware interfaces, all infrastructure is checked in, and any changes to it can be tracked. Like application code, all changes should be required to be reviewed and approved, another safeguard often not offered when hardware is manually configured.

SECRETS MANAGEMENT

To securely build a successful CI/CD pipeline, it is important to carefully manage credentials including usernames and passwords as well as private keys. Whether these be credentials used to connect the application to a data source or the credentials needed to automatically deploy infrastructure, these secrets must be carefully managed. These secrets cannot be stored in the source code repository, where they are easily discoverable by potential threat actors even if the source code is protected. In addition, similar to shared passwords, storing secrets in the source code repositories can lead to a lack of knowledge of who has access to which systems and easily give people access that they should not have. Even worse, these secrets are often inadvertently exposed on the open Internet for anyone to access.

Secrets management provides a set of tools to securely store any credentials and other sensitive information that can then be accessed by applications with the appropriate credentials. These secrets include passwords, API keys or credentials, and tokens or certificates. Common secrets management tools include Vault AWS Secrets Manager and Azure Key Vault. These tools enable many developers to leverage the same set of secrets without even knowing them or having access to them.

The following IaC example from HashiCorp uses their secrets manager, called Vault, to retrieve temporary credentials that are then used to create compute resources (EC2 instances) in AWS:

```
variable "name" { default = "dynamic-aws-creds-operator" }
variable "region" { default = "us-east-1" }
variable "path" { default = "../vault-admin-workspace/
terraform.tfstate" }
variable "ttl" { default = "1" }

terraform {
  backend "local" {
    path = "terraform.tfstate"
  }
}

data "terraform_remote_state" "admin" {
  backend = "local"

  config = {
    path = var.path
  }
}

data "vault_aws_access_credentials" "creds" {
  backend = data.terraform_remote_state.admin.outputs.
backend
  role    = data.terraform_remote_state.admin.outputs.role
```

```
}

provider "aws" {
  region     = var.region
  access_key = data.vault_aws_access_credentials.creds
.access_key
  secret_key = data.vault_aws_access_credentials.creds
.secret_key
}

data "aws_ami" "ubuntu" {
  most_recent = true

  filter {
    name   = "name"
    values = ["ubuntu/images/hvm-ssd/ubuntu-trusty-14.04-
amd64-server-*"]
  }

  filter {
    name   = "virtualization-type"
    values = ["hvm"]
  }

  owners = ["099720109477"] # Canonical
}

# Create AWS EC2 Instance
resource "aws_instance" "main" {
  ami           = data.aws_ami.ubuntu.id
  instance_type = "t2.nano"

  tags = {
    Name  = var.name
    TTL   = var.ttl
    owner = "${var.name}-guide"
  }
}
```
[4]

---

[4] Nguyen, Tu. "Build Infrastructure." GitHub. HashiCorp, July 13, 2020. https://
github.com/hashicorp/learn-terraform-inject-secrets-aws-
vault/blob/main/operator-workspace/main.tf#L20.

Privileged Access Management

Privileged access management (PAM) is a cybersecurity mechanism for protecting access to resources from databases to infrastructure to codebases. PAM provides monitoring and detection of unauthorized access as well as providing mechanisms for safely, allowing the right level of access to the appropriate users. There are several tools and combinations of tools that can aid in PAM. One of the benefits of PAM solutions is that they can allow temporary access just in time to a select user, thereby providing the minimal access required without preventing access that is needed. If an engineer needs access to a system to troubleshoot an incident, they can be granted temporary access to that system or to the set of impacted systems. Instead of providing blanket access for an indefinite period of time to a large group of users—as with older identity approaches—PAM solutions can allow temporary access. This aligns very well with the Zero Trust approaches to identity discussed in Chapter 2, "The Evolution of Cybersecurity (from Perimeter to Zero Trust").

A DevSecOps approach to PAM requires a new way of thinking about access management. While you still need to ensure people have the least privileges needed to do their job, you need to think carefully about enablement and empowerment. One of the best ways to disempower someone is to not give them the ability to execute their job or to require them to ask permission to do the basic tasks needed to do their job. It is important to stop thinking of security as a gate, and instead think of it as guardrails. PAM can be a powerful tool to allow people to have access to the systems they need in emergency situations, so it is very important that this access be quickly implemented. Instead of thinking about how to stop people from doing stupid things, start thinking about how to enable them to do their jobs in a safe way. While this is a subtle difference, it is critical when considering the approach to identity and access management.

In thinking about the implementation of PAM, it is important to consider the access that people need to do their jobs. If you are asking developers to be responsible for runtime security of the platforms and services they build, they need access to the security telemetry for those systems. If you are asking teams to be responsible for responding to incidents, you should empower them to easily push updates to resolve the issues. This is not to say that you simply allow everyone to have access to everything all the time. Quite the opposite. PAM gives you the ability to provide granular control for specified time windows. It also allows you to monitor more closely for dynamic indicators of compromised accounts. By leveraging all the capabilities of PAM, you can ensure that everyone can do their jobs seamlessly, without compromising security.

RUNTIME APPLICATION SELF-PROTECTION

Runtime application self-protection (RASP) tools are another powerful bullet in your DevSecOps arsenal for managing operational activities. RASP uses information about an application's internal state to identify potential threats at runtime, which may not have been identified earlier in the process. When RASP tools detect potential threats, they can automatically take action to address the threat. RASP leverages the internal application logic to detect potential attacks. Based on the attack, these tools can take actions—such as isolating, blocking, or alerting—to ensure that the attack is prevented.

RASP acts like an internal sensor similar to an internal motion sensor that might detect an intruder and sound an alert or automatically lock doors when intrusion is detected. Because RASP tools are built into the application, they have insight into the internal application execution, thus providing deeper visibility into what might constitute a threat. In addition, they can take an active role in defending against the attack. Because of the automated nature of RASP tools, they help eliminate toil and become an important part of the DevSecOps toolset.

MONITORING AND OBSERVABILITY

Monitoring and *observability* technologies are core to DevSecOps because these extend beyond Agile deployment into the operational aspect of a system. Monitoring and observability tools provide insight into potential system issues in near real time, allowing developers to detect security attacks before they impact their services. These tools also help them understand the scope of security incidents, identify the cause, and implement remediation as quickly as possible.

Monitoring

Monitoring is the process of observing how a system behaves. Monitoring relies on the *telemetry* of a system, where telemetry is defined as the data that is recorded and transmitted about how a system behaves. At a base level, this telemetry can include system-level metrics such as CPU levels. It can also include data from monitoring tools, such as endpoint detection and response (EDR), which sit on system endpoints and issue alerts when they detect potential security issues. In line with the concepts of Defense in Depth, security monitoring can and should sit at every layer of your application, from the database to the user experience. Monitoring should also include monitoring of your logs for patterns, which may be indicative of a security issue. Something as simple as a large spike in log messages about failed authorization may be indicative of an intrusion attempt.

One of the toughest challenges that many midsize to large enterprises face today is the massive growth of monitoring data and the proliferation of monitoring tools. With the increasing size and complexity of systems has come an increasing number of monitoring points and data about those points. In addition, there seems to be a never-ending flood of tools to help you monitor the security of your systems. However, this proliferation of tools and data points can actually be detrimental to your ability to rapidly identify real security threats and issues.

MONITORING TOOL PROLIFERATION

At one company I worked, we had more than 50 monitoring tools, from database to system to real user monitoring! At each layer, there were multiple tools duplicating the same type of monitoring. Not only that, but even where the same tools were

(continues)

(*continued*)

used, the implementation was different so that they could not be used in the same way. In one data center, alerts were arranged by application; in another they were arranged by rack number. On one tool a red alert meant something completely different than a red alert on another system.

Because of the number of tools and alerts, it was practically impossible to identify when an actual problem was occurring. Even with a modern *security operations center (SOC)* with a full wall display there was nowhere enough room to begin to look at all of the monitoring dashboards and information. Postmortems would often reveal that an alert had fired but that no one had seen it.

We undertook a massive effort to redefine our monitoring stack, looking for duplication and removing tools wherever possible. We rationalized the tools from 50 down to just 12. We also worked diligently to define standards so that monitoring tools were used in a uniform manner across all of the systems. The final step in the process was to identify and reduce alert noise. We created a rule that any alert must be acted upon, even if that action was to turn off the alert if it was not useful. With this effort, the team significantly improved its ability to detect and prevent potential threats and to drive resolutions quickly when problems did arise.

Because of the continued increasing size and complexity of systems, monitoring is rarely sufficient and quickly becomes unmanageable without additional tools to correlate and present the data. In some cases, telemetry in isolation can be of limited use. For example, CPU utilization data in isolation offers very little value as it may or may not have a bearing on system performance or customer experience. What does it tell you if the CPU is at 100 percent utilization? Is this a good thing or a bad thing? In some systems you may very well want to use the maximum available processing power, so higher CPU utilization may actually be an indicator of optimum performance. In other systems, it may be an indicator of a *Distributed-Denial-of-Service (DDoS)* attack. What matters most is the user experience, so it is critical to collaborate with users early in the development process to carefully define and monitor performance against these expectations. However, especially in cybersecurity, user experience alone is not enough because there may be no impact to user experience in the case of a breach or attempted breach.

Because of the proliferation of data sources, it is important to leverage tools to provide correlation and presentation of the data to rapidly identify and address potential security issues. Correlation takes the telemetry from many data sources and brings it together, helping to identify duplicates and potentially related events from separate systems. For example, CPU spiking alone may not be indicative of a problem, but CPU spiking in conjunction with alerts from network detection and response (NDR) system and increased response times from synthetic user monitoring may be indicative of a DDoS attack. *Security information and event management (SIEM)* tools such a Splunk and Datadog attempt to take all of the various data sources, correlate them, and present them in a way that is easily digestible and actionable by humans. Figure 5.2 provides a basic representation of a correlation tool, which takes data from many sources to provide a useful representation of the data via a presentation layer.

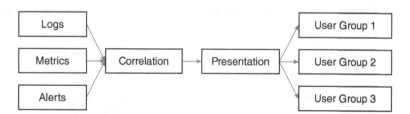

Figure 5.2   Correlating events across all logs, metrics, and alerts provides a variety of views for the many users of monitoring data.

Observability

Observability takes the next step in managing the operations of complex systems, as it focuses on answering novel questions about the current status of the system. *Observability* is a measure of how well internal states of a system can be inferred from knowledge of its external outputs. Monitoring and observability are distinct concepts that depend on each other. Monitoring is an action you perform to increase the observability of your system. Observability, on the other hand, is a property of that system, like stability or maintainability. One important difference between monitoring and observability is that monitoring requires you to know, in advance, what you want to know about. Because of the complexity of systems today, it is often impossible to predict what you will need to know about. Observability tools, on the other hand, allow you to ask new questions about the status of a system.

The concept of observability actually dates back to the 1960s when the concept was introduced by the Hungarian-American engineer Rudolf E. Kálmán, in the field of control theory, the mathematical study of systems, such as industrial processes. Kálmán states that a system was observable if its internal state could be inferred from the external outputs. In recent years, this same concept has been extended to technical applications and services.

The three pillars of observability are metrics, logs, and traces. These pillars can be understood as follows:

- **Metrics**—Metrics represent key-value pairs of information about a system. Metrics might include information such as the number of transactions per second or CPU utilization levels. This is often time-series data.

- **Logs**—Logs are representations of system status or events that are stored in a file.

- **Traces**—Traces represent the flow of activity through a system, with insight into each step a single transaction might take.

Each of these pillars has unique benefits as well as shortcomings. When the three pillars of observability are brought together, you can gain a wholistic picture of a system's performance. New Relic expanded on the idea with the MELT model, which includes metrics, events, logs, and traces, where events represent an action happening at a precise moment, such as when a system exceeds a specified threshold.

Data Silos

While DevSecOps often focuses on eliminating organizational and process silos, there are frequently data silos that underpin these organizational silos. In the field of security, the isolation of data can, at times, be necessary for confidentiality or privacy reasons. However, more often than not, these data silos are unnecessary and can impede the flow of information across the organization. You see these data silos when development teams have the data they are looking at, such as defects, and operations, has a separate set of data including things like log files or real user monitoring, and security has another set of data, such as vulnerability data and intrusion detection alerts. In addition, the business users often have a completely separate set of data that they are looking at, such as revenue or user conversion rates.

DATA SILOS' IMPACT ON INCIDENT RESOLUTION

I have all too often been on incident bridges and heard these data silos play out in real time with the security team looking at one set of metrics, the operations team looking at another, and the infrastructure teams looking at a completely separate set of information, with no team having visibility into the other team's data.

The network team will report, "We're not seeing any problem on our side."

The database team will report, "No issues on the database."

The development team will report, "Application is not reporting any errors."

But the incident managers, and, frequently, the customers, know there is a problem. However, the lack of transparency impairs collaboration, leading to lack of trust and delays in resolution.

The *DevOps Handbook* speaks about exactly these issues, stating, "for decades we have ended up with silos of information, where Development only creates logging events that are interesting to developers, and Operations only monitors whether the environments are up or down. As a result, when inopportune events occur, no one can determine why the entire system is not operating as designed or which specific component is failing, impeding our ability to bring our system back to a working state."[5] Unless these data silos are broken down, they will serve only to emphasize existing organizational silos. However, a proper approach and architecture for your monitoring data can help.

Fortunately, you can take steps to help eliminate data silos. One of the first steps is to fix the data coming in. One key step here is to look at the various inputs and reduce duplicate systems wherever possible. If there are two systems used for the same purpose, it is beneficial to eliminate one. This often happens in legacy systems, where previous functionality and data were used differently under different management or business features and not properly eliminated, modified, or turned off. While flexibility and autonomy are important in DevSecOps, this is one area where it can be beneficial to consolidate and align across the organization. This is not to say you should have one tool to do all the monitoring. At the same time, having five different tools to monitor the CPU is clearly also not ideal. While it is good to have generalizable tools that cover multiple types of monitoring, it is also important to identify key point solutions. You may, for example, require a specific tool for vulnerability management in your cloud environment separate from your data center environment. The number of tools and the focus of the tools will differ based on the size and maturity of an organization. What is important is that you reduce redundancy in your telemetry wherever possible.

Wherever possible, it is also important to drive consistency across your data sources. For tools that are part of the distributed tracing chain, you should make sure that the trace ID is included in metrics, logs, and alerts. In addition, key values such as application ID must be included in your data sources. If one tool refers to an application by ID

[5] Kim, Gene, Jez Humble, Patrick Debois, and John Willis. 2021. The DevOps Handbook: How to Create World-Class Agility, Reliability, & Security in Technology Organizations. 1st ed. Portland: IT Revolution Press.

and another uses another name, it will rapidly become difficult if not impossible to correlate the data across the disparate tools throughout the environment.

Once source data has been appropriately addressed, the data can be brought into a unified data store. The data store can be centralized or distributed depending on your size and the distribution of the application landscape. What is important is that you can leverage key data across all sources.

This same approach should be used for security. All too often, security data is siloed away in the name of "security," when the real intent is job security. Data is not shared as a way for individuals to maintain control and prevent others from easily replacing them. But you must share data carefully, as not all users should have access to all data. Transparency is good, but complete transparency could expose sensitive information about your vulnerabilities to malicious actors. Trust is also important, but insider threat is a reality so you need to ensure that sensitive data is exposed only to the right people. This can be accomplished by managing access to the data through access controls. When data is appropriately categorized, it can be segregated so that the appropriate people have access to the data they need. In this way, you can share data effectively across the organization to drive better collaboration without exposing vital security information.

Event Management with SIEM and SOAR

Because of the quantity of information that can be produced during production, SIEM tools can be used to collect all of the data and help security operations teams and security engineers use the data. As mentioned earlier, SIEM tools collect data from all of the sources of security-related information including logs, metrics, traces, and events to provide unified insight and management of this data. These tools provide real-time analysis of this data, helping make sense of the vast amount of information from monitoring and logging systems and helping identify potential attacks. SIEM tools can also assist in incident troubleshooting and response by identifying the cause of the incident and assisting with automation.

SIEM tools can detect a security incident and all of the alerts related to the incident and present it in a way that is easily actionable. For example, during a DoS-type attack, there may be hundreds or even thousands of alerts as systems try to respond to the flood of requests. SIEM tools can correlate these alerts and suppress duplicates, making it easier to diagnose the problem and drive a quicker resolution.

SOAR tools help automate many of these sorts of activities. SOAR refers to a collection of tools that help collect data on vulnerabilities and security events and automate the responses. These tools can be built to automatically respond to known threat types. If the preventative actions for certain types of attacks are known, these responses can be automated using SOAR. With the focus on increasing automation to reduce toil, SOAR tools can be an important part of the DevSecOps toolset.

CONCLUSION

While DevSecOps is not about technology, tools, CI/CD pipelines, and automation are essential to enabling the principles of DevOps within a security context. Build a culture of collaboration—tools alone do not make you "DevOps."

Build a culture of collaboration—tools alone do not make you "DevOps."

DevOps focuses on the CI/CD pipeline because it enables small batch delivery, which, in turn, allows for the flow of value to the customer, shorter feedback loops, and experimentation, *all* of the Three Ways of DevOps. By integrating security into the CI/CD pipeline, you can extend the benefits of DevOps to security, thus enabling the DevSecOps culture.

When you use privileged access management and secrets management correctly, you empower engineers with the access they need to do their jobs quickly and efficiently, ensuring they aren't blockers. In doing so, you enable a state of flow in the creative process of developing great technology, which is critical to building the best products and systems on Earth (and the universe!).

Monitoring and observability provide key components in the transparency of the DevOps culture. If you want to move from a paradigm where the security team is solely responsible for security to one where security is everyone's responsibility, you must give everyone visibility into the data about security which is so critical to making good decisions about security. While you must be careful about sharing confidential information, sharing information about vulnerabilities in a transparent way across all technology teams can be a great way to drive improvement in those areas.

Automation helps free engineers from manual tasks, enabling them to focus on higher-level engineering problems. SIEM and SOAR can significantly reduce operational overhead, thus automating the most common activities in security engineering. In addition, this automation can help reduce the noise from monitoring telemetry to help focus on the important signals that indicate valid security threats.

Through technology, you enable the culture of DevOps. Automation can help drive greater flow of value to your customers, as can your CI/CD pipelines. By building security automation, you can ensure that security is done as part of everything your organization does instead of being added on as an afterthought.

CHAPTER 6

DevSecOps Governance

INTRODUCTION

Governance seeks to ensure the compliance of an organization with policies designed to protect that organization. Governance, risk, and compliance is a rapidly growing area of concern for many companies due to the rapidly shifting compliance standards. Traditional methods of governance and compliance have been highly manual, relying on controls listed in spreadsheets and evidence manually produced and delivered. DevSecOps brings a new approach to governance, risk, and compliance that can help save manual effort from engineers while improving compliance through automation.

Governance does not, in and of itself, bring value to customers. However, governance does ensure that companies comply with regulations and policies that are designed to limit systemic risk. This compliance, in turn, provides validation to customers that those risk mitigation activities have been adhered to and, in doing so, builds trust with customers and other regulating bodies. It is certainly possible, especially for smaller companies, to be secure without governance. However, as companies grow and become more complex, this governance helps ensure that companies are behaving in a way that mitigates known risks.

DevSecOps brings an automated approach to compliance with *compliance as code* and governance automation, which can be immensely powerful for companies. Compliance as code is a methodology for automating compliance tasks by describing themes in a programmatic fashion. Compliance as code can include activities such as defining controls in code and automatically verifying that infrastructure and applications adhere to these controls as part of your deployment pipeline.

In the same way that inserting automated security testing in your CI/CD pipeline helps you produce code, which is more secure while reducing manual efforts, compliance as code can help you comply with audit requirements. By implementing your compliance verification in an automated way, you can significantly improve your adherence to compliance standards, reduce the time your engineers spend on compliance-related tasks, and increase your time to market.

THE CHALLENGE OF COMPLIANCE

The work involved in maintaining compliance for public companies cannot be underestimated. Legislation and regulation in the last 20 years has substantially increased the amount of work that public companies need to do to ensure compliance. In addition, to maintain compliance, engineers often make extensive manual efforts, pulling them away from the critical task of developing products and services for their customers.

The History of Compliance

Compliance requirements for corporations in the United States date back to the early 19th century and have accelerated significantly through the 20th century. Compliance regulations and regulating bodies have arisen in response to corporate misdeeds and public scandals and the negative impact on the broader economy. Regulations in the United States around public companies go as far back as the Interstate Commerce Act of 1887 and the Sherman Antitrust Act of 1890. However, it wasn't until the 20th century that modern compliance really arose with the launch of the Food and Drug Administration (FDA) in 1906.

The 2000s gave birth to much of what developers focus on in modern compliance with the launch of the Sarbanes-Oxley Act (SOX) in 2002 and the Payment Card Industry (PCI) in 2006. The Sarbanes-Oxley Act was created in response to public corporate scandals in the United States with Enron and WorldCom, which led the Securities and Exchange Commission (SEC) to define regulations for how public companies needed to operate and report on their finances.

The Payment Card Industry standards were created by a group of financial services companies—including MasterCard, Visa, and American Express—to address cybersecurity threats to payment systems. Today companies must comply with a wide range of compliance regulations, including SOX, HIPAA, FedRAMP, EU Model Contracts, and SEC Reg-SCI regulations, as well as contractual obligations, such as PCI DSS or DOD DISA.

COMPLIANCE CHALLENGES

At one company I had just started working for, we faced huge compliance hurdles. Because of our inability to show compliance with SOX audit requirements for two years in a row, we were at risk of having a significant deficiency and potentially even a material weakness, which would need to be made public via SEC filings. Just two months into a new job and I found myself in a SOX compliance war room. I don't know if you've ever been in a war room, but they are generally some of the toughest high-pressure situations anyone can imagine, and a SOX compliance war room was likely one of the most painful experiences of my career.

We spent two weeks meeting with team after team to review their evidence, ask questions, and schedule follow-up meetings to get additional information. Team after team came in to present their evidence of compliance around access and change governance.

One team showed their change approvals, documented via email, bringing in, as evidence, long email threads with approvals at the bottom. Other teams showed tickets pulled from Jira, others still from ServiceNow. Some had policies documented in Word, others in email. Engineers were spending hours and hours of their time just digging around to provide manual documentation, matching it to server logs showing

(continues)

(continued)

actual change deployment related to the change approval. We spent a full two weeks in the war room, and the engineers spent a staggering amount of time outside of that room running around trying to find the right evidence to show compliance.

What this effort illustrated was that disparate and manual processes, managed through varying manual processes, was costing the company millions of dollars and putting the company at serious risk of violating compliance regulations.

Over the next two years, we took steps to develop our compliance as code approach. Our first steps were to unify our processes and our tracking. This fell into two major categories— change management and identity and access management.

We built an adaptive change management process to be used for modern applications with sophisticated deployment processes as well as for legacy applications that had, until then, manual and tightly coordinated steps. Over the next nine months we rolled this process out across all of our teams.

We implemented three new systems to manage identity and access controls. We implemented Azure AD to provide internal users access to the applications and services they needed. We deployed CyberArk for privileged access management to ensure that only the right people had access to privileged accounts and then only for the set time periods needed. And we implemented Saviynt to manage identity governance, ensuring the right roles in the organization had access to the systems they needed and only those systems. This allowed us to deprecate legacy IGA systems, reduce complexity in our system, and provide more secure access for our users.

We also created governance, risk, and compliance tooling to track all of the compliance regulations that we were required to meet. With this foundation set across all of our systems, we

(*continued*)

had a stable base to work from. We were able to begin to map controls in Saviynt to the evidence that was required to prove those controls. Because everyone was now following the same processes and using the same tools, repeating tests for different applications was simple. We were able to automate what had previously been hundreds of hours of manual effort in evidence collection and significantly improve our compliance. During this time, we reduced our IT general control deficiencies from 66 to just 4 minor deficiencies and eliminated the burden of manual evidence collection, allowing our engineers to focus on building products and services.

The Burden of Compliance

Maintaining compliance is a huge cost for public companies. This includes the cost of internal and external auditors, regulatory filing fees, and costs for the systems required to manage compliance. These costs extend to technical teams as well. Engineers must spend countless hours ensuring that the systems they are building comply with regulations. In addition, they must spend time tracking and reporting on evidence of compliance. A 2021 study of the costs of compliance for public companies found that the cost of compliance was 4.1 percent of the market capitalization for the median U.S. public company.[1] A separate survey conducted by the Risk Management Association found that 50 percent of respondents said they spent between 6 and 10 percent of their revenue on compliance costs. Whichever way you cut it, these are huge numbers.

The fines for noncompliance are even larger. In 2010, the SEC assessed a $550 million fine against Goldman Sachs for misleading investors about a subprime mortgage product linked to the collapse of the U.S. housing market in 2008. In 2017, Deutsche Bank was fined

---

[1] Ewens, Michael, Kairong Xiao, and Ting Xu. "Regulatory Costs of Being Public: Evidence from Bunching Estimation." National Bureau of Economic Research, (2021). https://doi.org/10.3386/w29143.

£163 million by the UK regulatory body the Financial Conduct Authority (FC) for failing to properly protect information about customer relationships. These fines are not limited to financial institutions. In 2019 the Federal Trade Commission (FTC) imposed a $5 billion penalty on Facebooks' parent company Meta for failing to protect the privacy of users' personal information.

Not only that, but the way in which compliance is implemented in companies often limits a company's agility and adaptability. When compliance is managed as a set of manual checks that gate releases to production, it means additional work and rework every time new features and functionalities are brought to market. In addition, manual compliance audits postproduction mean substantial effort must be spent manually collecting evidence and remediating audit findings. A Garner survey found that 81 percent of IT professionals feel that InfoSec policies inhibit speed and agility.[2] Not only that, but of those surveyed, 77 percent of information security professionals agree. So, not only do engineers see this impact but cybersecurity professionals agree.

MANAGING RISK

Ultimately all cybersecurity work should be understood as an effort to manage risk. Governance and compliance are steps that help ensure that risk-mitigation activities are undertaken. Governance provides the overarching framework while compliance ensures that specified steps are taken within that framework. Many elements comprise a business's risk profile. Cybersecurity is only one element, but it is the focus for this book. Most public companies have complete *Enterprise Risk Management (ERM)* programs that evaluate all the potential risks, as these must be reported in the company's quarterly filings. As cybersecurity is a growing risk for almost all companies today, a DevSecOps approach can be hugely helpful in mitigating these risks.

The goal of cybersecurity is not to eliminate risk but to manage it. Ultimately, you can never completely eliminate risk, but you can

---

[2] Proctor, Paul, Greg Young, Sid Deshpande, Jeremy D'Hoinne, and Ray Wagner. "Predicts 2016: Threat and Vulnerability Management." Gartner Research, (2016).

significantly reduce it. That reduction must be in balance with a company's risk tolerance. It is possible for a company to spend almost infinite amounts of money mitigating cybersecurity risk and still not be 100 percent risk free. It is, therefore, important to consider the cost and benefit of cybersecurity efforts to mitigate risk. The governance frameworks should help align these efforts with the compliance requirements and the risk tolerance for that business.

The correct risk levels for a business are dependent on many aspects of that business, including size, industry, and stage of development. A small company trying to get a new product to market quickly may have a higher risk tolerance because it values development of new features over mitigating risk. Because of the lower number of users, a new company may not have the same risk exposure of a larger, more established player. In addition, if a startup cannot get the features it needs to its initial users, security may not matter at all if the company fails. On the other hand, established companies with highly sensitive data—such as financial and healthcare information—have a much lower risk tolerance and do all they can to mitigate cybersecurity risk.

Risk as a Feature

With a DevSecOps approach, risk should be thought of as another feature. In this way, risk-based activities should be placed on teams' backlogs and prioritized and managed through each development team's queues just as other features are. You should pay careful attention to these risk features, as these are all too often deprioritized in favor of feature work. Ultimately, if a system is not resilient and secure, it will not matter if it has all the flashy features in the world. As examples like Medstar Health and Telefonica make clear, forgoing cybersecurity risk can be the downfall of many a promising company. This priority must be clear through the training of development and product managers alike.

Tracking the amount of risk work helps provide visibility into whether the right amount of effort is going to risk mitigation efforts. In his book *Project to Product*, Mik Kersten introduces the concept of flow metrics, which provide a great mechanism for measuring risk-based work. *Project to Product* provides a way of measuring the pace of delivery as well as the types of work being done in the development life cycle. He breaks work down into four key types: Feature, Defect, Risk, and Debt. By implementing this type of measurement through tagging work items, you can see how much work is dedicated to risk mitigation activities, from remediating vulnerabilities to meeting regulatory requirements to implementing new security features. All of this can and should be viewed and prioritized as a feature of the product.

Risk Management and Controls

Many levels of risk exist, from enterprise risks such as market shifts to individual risk items such as a vulnerability on a specific cloud instance. It is useful to understand the structures of risk management and how they relate. A good risk management program includes many items:

- **Risk framework**—Risk frameworks such as NIST and COBIT provide a structure for risk management.

- **Compliance standards**—There are many standards (such as SOX and PCI) that you may have to comply with, depending on your company's size and structure. Standards that companies must adhere to depend on industry, business size, business type, and the types of activities the business is involved in.

- **Policy**—Policies are written documents that help you comply with the frameworks or standards with which you need to comply.

- **Controls**—Controls are actions that are in place to ensure that you comply with the policy as written.

- **Evidence**—Evidence is the proof that a control has been met.

- **Attestation**—This is the signed and dated evidence where the responsible party acknowledges that the evidence satisfies the control.

While many different cybersecurity frameworks exist, Figure 6.1 highlights the fact that there is significant overlap between them.

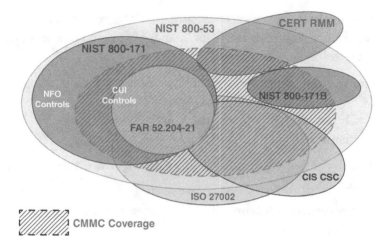

Figure 6.1 The different cybersecurity frameworks have significant areas of overlap.

Risk and privacy standards have similar overlaps. With emerging privacy standards, for example, many different standards exist. However, there is significant overlap here as well, as illustrated in Figure 6.2.

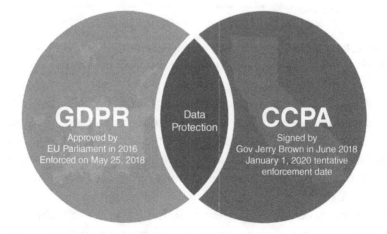

Figure 6.2 Standards such as the emerging standards for the protection of privacy also have areas of overlap.

Policies help set rules to ensure that the requirements of the frameworks are adopted and legal standards are met. The controls then act as tests of these standards.

Controls are generally broken down into three main categories:

- **Detective**—A control that indicates when a risk has already manifested

- **Corrective**—A control that repairs the process to compensate for a risk

- **Preventive**—A control that makes the risk less likely to manifest

Once the controls are established, evidence must then be collected to show that the standards are met. Generally, you can think of the connection between frameworks, standards, policies, controls, and evidence, as outlined in Figure 6.3.

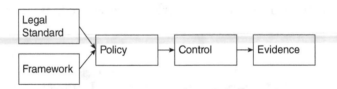

Figure 6.3 The hierarchy of risk management flows from general standards and frameworks to specific controls and evidence of those controls.

For example, NIST recommends a password policy that requires all user-created passwords to be at least eight characters in length, and all machine-generated passwords to be at least six characters in length. A company may then have a policy that all passwords are at least 12 characters in length, with upper- and lowercase letters, numbers, and symbols. Controls for this policy might include rules within the Identity and Access Management tool. Evidence might include a random set of users and passwords sampled from the user base. In this way, the controls enforce the guidelines created in the frameworks and legal standards that a company must adhere to.

It should be noted that policies may map to multiple frameworks and standards and that the controls may also map to multiple policies.

While this may add confusion, it can be a good thing because one control may help drive compliance to multiple standards.

DevSecOps Approach to Governance

DevSecOps requires a fundamentally different approach to governance. A DevSecOps approach means increased collaboration between auditors, cybersecurity practitioners, site reliability engineers, and developers. The governance, risk, and compliance practitioners and internal auditors should be working side-by-side with developers so that the developers can better understand the audit requirements. The audit teams can also better understand how developers are specifically meeting the requirements. You should work to break down the silos between these teams and find opportunities for collaboration. By understanding each other's goals, all teams can design better solutions.

Tighter collaboration provides opportunities to shift governance to the left in the process. By involving governance and audit teams earlier in the process, you can ensure that the design team meets the requirements rather than discovering them at the end of the process and having to remediate after release.

In addition, a DevSecOps approach to governance means that you should find opportunities to automate and reduce toil. Traditional governance processes entail spreadsheets for tracking controls and extensive manual efforts for tracking evidence. These processes require significant time and effort to manually track down and upload compliance evidence. The following sections of this chapter detail ways to automate this process to reduce manual work and increase the velocity of delivery.

Compliance as Code

The good news is that a compliance as code approach can help you significantly reduce the burden discussed in the previous section. Compliance as code attempts to describe compliance requirements in a programmatic language so that compliance activities can be automated.

There is an increasingly wide array of tools to help you do this. Compliance as code can be inserted as several points throughout the development life cycle—at build time, at runtime, as well as during audits—to show evidence of compliance.

Build-Time Compliance as Code

Following "Shift Left" principles, these compliance as code practices can be executed earlier in the development life cycle to increase the rate of feedback to developers and reduce the friction in addressing compliance requirements. By inserting automated compliance verification when developers check in their application or infrastructure code, you can catch issues earlier and provide immediate feedback. As with vulnerability scanning, this practice can be integrated directly into the IDE to further reduce the feedback cycle. In the blog for the configuration management vendor Chef, they write that "Compliance has both a build-time and a runtime component," and you learn about each of these in the following sections.

Inserting Compliance into the Pipeline

In the same way that DevSecOps builds security into the CI/CD pipeline, compliance automation and tooling can be integrated to reduce the overall cost of compliance without slowing down product delivery. This practice aligns with the principles of Shift Left by ensuring that the code meets compliance regulations when it is checked in or built rather than trying to check for compliance after the project is completed and the system is deployed.

You should use the same tools to ensure the security of your pipeline as you do to secure the code you are building with the pipeline. This means using infrastructure as code for any components of your pipeline infrastructure and checking in the code for the pipeline configuration into your source code repository. You also need to ensure that all the tools you use to secure your applications and services, from SAST to endpoint security, are used on the pipeline itself.

Compliance Automation

While security tools have been around for a long time, at this point the set of compliance automation tools is still very much in its infancy. However, a set of standards and new set of tools are rapidly emerging.

OPA/Rego

Open Policy Agent (OPA) and *Rego* are key sources for defining policies in a unified language. OPA is an open-source engine that allows you to define policies. It allows you to define policies as code, and it has been adopted as a standard by many other tools. Rego is the declarative language that supports OPA. It is used to describe OPA policies in an easily understandable format.

In this simple example from OPA, they use Rego to describe a policy for an application that prevents anyone except a pet's owner from updating their pet's name:

```
package application.authz
import future.keywords
# Only owner can update the pet's information
# Ownership information is provided as part of OPA's input
default allow := false

allow if {
        input.method == "PUT"
        some petid
        input.path = ["pets", petid]
        input.user == input.owner
}
```[3]

In this way, you can express your policies as code. One of the major benefits of OPA and Rego is that they separate the policy

---

[3] "Policy-based Control for Cloud Native Environments." Open Policy Agent. Accessed April 24, 2023. www.openpolicyagent.org.

definition from the code of the infrastructure of the application. So, if a policy changes, you can easily update the Rego code without having to modify the applications that rely on it.

Runtime Compliance as Code

As you verify that the code you developed for production is compliant with rules and regulations, it is also important to examine the runtime environment. As Julian Dunn notes in the Chef blog, "Compliance has both a build-time and a runtime component." Although the checked-in code may be compliant, there may be interactions between disparate code segments that violate compliance regulations. In addition, there may be components of the system, such as user roles, that are not managed as code and never pushed throughout the deployment pipeline. It is therefore equally important that you take a programmatic approach to verifying runtime environments as well.

Compliance as Code for Auditing

In addition to integrating compliance into your development pipeline, you should look for ways to automate the process of control mapping and evidence collection to lessen the burden of audits. While ensuring compliance for deployed infrastructure and code is critical, it is not sufficient. You must also verify that those controls are working. For example, while you may have a rule that prevents passwords from being written directly into configuration code that is deployed through the pipeline, it may be possible for someone to circumvent this by manually deploying that infrastructure. So, it is important that you also verify that the controls in place in the development pipeline are having the intended effect. By taking a programmatic approach to control mapping and evidence collection, you can further reduce the cost of compliance on the resources and agility of an organization.

Many governance, risk, and compliance systems can help with this process. Systems such as ServiceNow and Saviynt can help map the standards to the policy to the control. Once you determine the evidence needed to prove that a control is adhered to, you can then automate the collection of that evidence and store it in an evidence repository. These evidence repositories should be immutable. Immutable repositories cannot be changed after creation, which will ensure that evidence cannot be tampered with. Once the evidence is collected, the controls can be marked as passing with links to the evidence. In this way, it is possible to eliminate the manual effort of evidence collection, making the process more secure and reliable for the auditors.

The Role of Audit

Beyond compliance as code for auditing, DevSecOps requires a fundamental shift in the audit approach. Traditionally, IT auditing has been based on a segregation of duties. The concept that operations and development are different teams, with different incentives, has provided the foundation for risk mitigation approaches for many years. Because these teams had separate focuses and reporting structures, it was assumed that the segregation of duties would provide appropriate checks and balances. Of course, this segregation of duties is contrary to the focus of DevOps, which strives to bring Dev and Ops together, thus building teams that have responsibility for building, deploying, and maintaining their codes.

As discussed in Chapter 3, "DevSecOps People," empowered engineers must have the ability to deploy and manage their systems if they are going to be held accountable for the availability and reliability of those systems. In addition, the CI/CD pipeline and the automation of change management fly in the face of traditional controls, which mandate layers of review and approval.

In 2015, James DeLuccia IV, Jeff Gallimore, Gene Kim, and Byron Miller wrote the *DevOps Audit Defense Toolkit*, in which they explore the challenges between audit and DevOps. They describe the problem statement:

> *"As IT organizations increasingly adopt DevOps patterns, there is more tension than ever between IT and audit. These new DevOps patterns challenge traditional thinking about auditing, controls, and risk mitigation. Just as 'Dev' and 'Ops' need to find new and better ways of working together to help their organization win, so now does IT and audit."*

The new ways of working in DevOps require a new way of thinking about auditing.

A Note of Caution on Compliance

It should be noted that compliance does not, in and of itself, make you secure. Compliance verifies that you meet specific standards aimed at preventing specific types of issues, but it does not guarantee security. Compliance does checks for security, but it doesn't necessarily make you secure. Cybersecurity is context dependent and constantly changing. The threat landscape is evolving much quicker than compliance regulations. You need to design your security posture based on the threat landscape and the business requirements of your company. Ideally this goes well above and beyond the requirements of compliance.

COMPLIANCE FOUNDATIONS

A key foundation to driving compliance as code automation is the need to have consistency. Having disparate processes and tool proliferation can make compliance significantly more complex to manage. IAM and the change management process stand as the foundation for many compliance requirements, so having consistency in these areas is of particular import. By driving standardization in these areas, you can significantly reduce the cost of compliance management and enable automation.

Identity and Access Management

Identity and Access Management (IAM) is at the core of modern cybersecurity. It is a key element of Zero Trust because it is the verified identity of the user that allows you to establish trust in the actions the user (or machine) wants to take with that identity. Keep in mind that IAM applies to systems as well as machines. It allows systems to interact with one another as well as users to interact with systems. In a Zero Trust model, if the identity cannot be securely and effectively established, that actor should not be allowed to take the action.

As decryption and hacking have become increasingly sophisticated, traditional methods of identity verification have had to evolve. A recent report by Hive Systems showed that it takes just one second to crack a seven letter password.[4] Even quite complex passwords can be cracked relatively easily with modern computing power. So it is incumbent upon companies to take increasingly sophisticated approaches to IAM.

Almost all companies today are using dual-factor authentication, which requires more than one way of establishing your identity, and, increasingly, companies are moving away from passwords altogether. Modern identity can be dynamic and based on historical data such as location and time of access. If a user is accessing systems at 2 a.m., when they normally work 9 to 5, this can indicate a problem. Systems can also look for impossible travel. If a user accessed a system from California one second and one from Nigeria one hour later, this is likely an indication that the account has been compromised. Modern identity systems should take into account all of these factors as part of the actor's identity. IAM is an increasingly complex topic—whole books have been written on the topic—and it is not the purpose of this book to explore IAM in detail. The purpose here is to provide an overview and put IAM in the context of DevSecOps and automated governance.

One of the keys for making IAM and DevSecOps successful is to ensure they are standardized across the organization. This is one of the foundational elements of governance, so standardization provides enormous benefits in terms of reducing manual overhead of managing separate identity systems. In addition, a centralized and standardized IAM makes it tremendously easier to provide people with the right levels of access to be most effective. Access can be very difficult to manage when separate systems have separate mechanisms for access. If your legacy CRM system has separate access controls from your cloud-based applications and that is separate from your ticketing system, managing these in any sort of holistic way can be next to impossible. That leaves you with significant risk.

---

[4] "Hive Systems Password." Hive Systems. Accessed April 24, 2023. www.hivesystems.io/password-table.

In addition, if systems are managed in a decentralized manner, it can be difficult, if not impossible, to provide a holistic audit for the organization to ensure that those who should have access do and those who should not do not. If there are multiple points at which identity can be managed, the burden for governance can be overwhelming. The process for identifying who has access to which systems alone can be a massive undertaking. When you have a centralized IAM system, you have a single point to check that the right people have access to the right systems. As IAM is central to compliance requirements, having a unified approach is key to any governance automation.

Change Management

Change management is another foundational element of DevSecOps. As discussed in Chapter 4, "DevSecOps Process," most change management processes have their roots in ITIL. Many of these processes are highly bureaucratic, with large documentation requirements and change advisory boards (CABs) required to review and approve all changes. Considering DevOps, this should be approached in a fundamentally different way, with changes recorded and approvals automated whenever possible. Change reviews should be localized to people who are technically familiar with the changes that are being made. This type of approach empowers engineers and enables flow unimpeded by bureaucratic overhead. In addition, when you properly insert security into the pipeline, it can lead to a more secure product.

Unfortunately, this approach flies in the face of conventional assumptions about change management. While many of these assumptions were designed before CI/CD was even a possibility, these assumptions are baked into policies and controls of many organizations. Many change-management policies are built on the assumption that there is a segregation of duties between development and operations teams and that this segregation of duties ensures that secure code will be released. It may be necessary to work closely with the audit team to review and update company policies for new approaches to change management to be acceptable.

The reality is that security is much better served having review from developers close to the code than having approval from a vice president working three layers above the person writing the code. In addition, an automated deployment pipeline designed with security engineers with security verification built in will be more secure than any manual review.

However, this may not align with the organization's policies. This issue is explored in *The DevOps Audit Defense Toolkit* by the fictitious auditors who had concerns that "the absence of separation of duty and change approval controls create the risk of untested and unauthorized code being introduced into production." That's okay, because there's a little-known fact: organizational policies can change.

This is not to say that *Separation of Duties (SoD)* is not a valid concept and not necessary to mitigate risk. SoD is the requirement that two separate parties be responsible for different parts of a process. Payroll is a good example. Often it is required that one person schedule the payroll and another person approve it. This helps ensure that no one person can do something like pay themselves twice. SoD is a foundation of modern risk management and ensures that no single bad actor can act in a vacuum to take malicious action. Traditional policies relied on the segregation of duties between development and operations to ensure that malicious code was not released. But DevOps fundamentally shifts this paradigm with the combination of Development and Operations, the elimination of CABs, and the automation of the approval pipeline.

However, it is quite possible to provide this sort of separation of duties in a DevOps environment. One of the key ways to achieve this is to ensure that all code is reviewed by someone other than the code submitter. This should be a requirement of all CI/CD pipelines and helps ensure that no single person can insert malicious code.

In addition, elevated access should be removed to ensure that the only way to deploy code to product systems is through the CI/CD pipeline. They reiterate this mitigation technique in *Investments Unlimited: A Novel about DevOps, Security, Audit Compliance, and Thriving in the Digital Age* by Helen Beal, Bill Bensing, Jason Cox, Michael

Edenzon, Topo Pal, Caleb Queern, John Rzezotarski, Andres Vega, and John Willis, stating "If we take away elevated production access from every developer and ensure that every code change is peer reviewed before production deployment, we will have the best way to mitigate that risk. . . . The key is enforcing the peer review process."

Additional controls can be added here to strengthen this control, such as including multiple reviewers and requiring rotation or randomization of code reviewers to prevent two people from teaming up to submit malicious code. While this may feel strange and risky to some, the reality is that a code reviewer familiar with the code is much more likely to catch subtle code changes that might be written with mal intent than a security or operations person who has never seen the code before.

In addition, by taking this approach, you shift the verification left and can catch any problems very early in the development process, rather than waiting until it is about to be deployed, or worse, it is running in production.

The other piece to keep in mind is that, by automating the security testing in the pipeline, you provide another control point in which to catch any problematic code. This sort of automated testing is likely to be more reliable and effective than manual testing, which would otherwise be necessary.

The DevOps *Audit Defense Toolkit* describes this risk and the related mitigating control as follows:

"Business Risk R1. An internal actor abuses provided or developed privileges to commit fraud to the organization and/or its customers. (BR2, BR3)

Control Strategy CS1. All code is validated through defined controls prior to production deployment to prevent developers from inserting 'back doors' or vulnerabilities into production."

The paper provides details about potential mitigating strategies including reviews and automation.

Ultimately, segregation of duties should not be a barrier to DevSecOps adoption. It is quite possible to segregate duties with automated deployments and peer reviews. However, in many environments, this may require a fundamentally different understanding and approach. It will require building a new shared understanding between security and auditing, which is understanding the risks and controls in place to mitigate these risks. It may even require that policies be rewritten if they explicitly call out a separation between development and operations.

The thing to keep in mind is that auditors and cybersecurity professionals share a common goal: they all want to reduce risk for the company. It is not the auditors' goal to make life difficult for engineers nor is it their desire to spend weeks and months filling in spreadsheets and manually pouring through evidence. Nor is it security's goal to slow down the product development process or create additional work for developers and site reliability engineers. Both groups are keenly focused on the goal of reducing risk. With that in mind, it is possible to agree on the best action to reduce risk and build that approach into policies and controls for the organization.

Conclusion

Governance automation is one of the biggest opportunities in DevSecOps. This area alone can save companies millions of dollars. Not only that, but governance automation can help ensure that engineers spend more time focused on building great products and services and less time in the manual toil of evidence collection and manual compliance activities. Yet it remains one of the most underdeveloped areas. While many companies are now adopting DevSecOps practices, they have yet to even begin their journey on governance automation.

A key to governance automation is, of course, collaboration. It is critical that you build collaboration with internal and external partners and view them as just that—partners, rather than a policing organization. You must build bridges between auditing, security, development, and site reliability engineering to be successful in your compliance automation efforts. It is important to remember that these teams may have different focuses and approaches. However, they are ultimately aligned on mitigating risks for the business.

It is also important to create a strong foundation for governance automation. Change management and IAM stand at the core of many compliance requirements. If you can do these two things well and in a standardized way across your organization, it will position you well to take your governance automation journey.

On top of this foundation, you can build your governance automation and tooling. New tools are emerging at a rapid pace to assist with your governance automation. Your CI/CD pipeline will play a central role, as many of the compliance requirements can be verified during the deployment process using common frameworks like Rego and OPA. Additional automation can be wrapped around your environments to map risks to controls and controls to evidence. That way, you can seamlessly verify that you are compliant, thus helping to ensure the security of your systems.

CHAPTER 7

Driving Transformation in Enterprise Environments

INTRODUCTION

More than 50 percent of the Fortune 500 companies from the year 2000 no longer exist.[1] In just two decades, more than half of the top 500 companies have disappeared. In many cases, the reason these companies no longer exist is a failure to transform, a failure to adapt to changing business conditions. The world is transforming, and your business must transform too if you want to continue to succeed. DevSecOps is one of the many transformations that businesses are going through today to meet the business needs of today and tomorrow.

As mentioned in Chapter 1, "Introducing DevSecOps," when approaching transformation, it is important to start with the "why." Transformation is hard. It is hard for the organizations, and it is hard for the people going through those transformations. Transformation is difficult because, to transform, you must fundamentally change not only what you are working on but how you work. Changing habits and ways of work—changing the way people work—is one of the most difficult challenges a business can face. If you are going through that difficulty, it is important to understand the underlying reason. By understanding and communicating the "why," you can help everyone in the organization become part of, and support, that transformation.

One of the primary factors for business transformation is quite simply to deliver better business results. For DevSecOps, this includes delivering secure products and services that the customers and market

---

[1] Berman, Ryan. "Business Apocalypse: Fifty-two Percent of Fortune 500 Companies from the Year 2000 Are Extinct." Courageous. April 24, 2020. `https://ryanberman` `.com/glossary/business-apocalypse`.

demand while outpacing the competition. It is important to go beyond platitudes to actually define how you measure these results and track progress as you go through this transformation. If your goal is to increase security while reducing time to market, you can look at metrics around security incidents, risk, and cycle time. Chapter 8, "Measuring DevSecOps," provides a detailed approach to measuring the progress of a DevSecOps transformation, but it is fundamentally about increasing value delivered to your customers. Ensuring risk reduction is part of that value delivery equation.

It is also important to keep in mind the forces that drive transformation. Technology is progressing more rapidly than ever in human history. Computer technology is now progressing more each hour than it did in the first 90 years.[2] To keep up with the rapid pace of technological change and to take advantage of it, you need to fundamentally change too. You need to fundamentally change your systems, processes, personnel, and even hierarchical organization. While this requires investments of time and money, the benefits far outweigh the costs, and not changing can lead to failure.

Not only must businesses do things in new ways to adopt new technology, but those new technologies also allow businesses to do things in new and better ways. As discussed in Chapter 2, "The Evolution of Cybersecurity (from Perimeter to Zero Trust)," the migration from compiled fully functional applications that were distributed on CD-ROM to Internet-based applications and software as a service has allowed for the move to continuous integration and continuous deployment. The tools that have emerged to allow companies to deploy continuously provide a unique challenge and a unique opportunity for cybersecurity. By integrating security into your continuous integration and continuous deployment pipeline, you can ensure that every release is secure and that security is built into how you work.

Emerging technologies such as artificial intelligence and Big Data provide new ways to protect systems, and you must take advantage of them. By leveraging Big Data and machine learning in your

---

[2] Grossman, Lev. "2045: The Year Man Becomes Immortal." Time, February 10, 2011.

monitoring and observability systems, you can now look at massive amounts of data from all of your systems and automatically identify patterns that may be indicative of security compromise.

THE CHALLENGE OF CULTURAL TRANSFORMATION

To successfully drive transformation, it is important to first understand the challenges that an organization faces during transformation so that these challenges can be handled head-on to drive a successful DevSecOps transformation.

Changing the way people work, how they are valued, how you communicate with them, what new tasks they will be asked to do, how they report their results, and how their roles may be redefined are the most difficult parts of any transformation. Changing tools or changing technologies, while not easy, is relatively straightforward in comparison. There are known patterns that you can leverage and, especially when using vendor-supplied technologies, there are people with prior experience who can help. As with other transformations, DevSecOps is, more than anything, a cultural transformation. You must make an effort to understand the current culture and the changes that need to be made to accommodate the culture you are aiming for.

Changing the way people work, how they are valued, how you communicate with them, what new tasks they will be asked to do, how they report their results, and how their roles may be redefined are the most difficult parts of any transformation. Changing tools or changing technologies, while not easy, is, in comparison, relatively straightforward.

Resistance to Change

Security has typically been performed in a silo, and this silo served a purpose, as there is often a requirement of secrecy for security. When a vulnerability is discovered, you cannot tell everyone, "Hey, guess what? We found a huge vulnerability!" Exposing this information can put a company at additional risk from malicious actors who might exploit the vulnerability. However, this approach is often contradictory to the DevOps culture of openness and transparency. So, you need to work to find the right balance. Confidentiality and secrecy have long been part of the culture of security, so finding the ability to be open about mistakes may be counterintuitive to many security professionals.

In addition, change introduces risk, and transformation represents a massive change, so transformation may be counter to the nature of many security professionals. Security professionals have spent their entire careers working to reduce risk. In many cases, they have made a conscious decision to make risk reduction their life's work. In the *Computer Weekly* article "It's time for engineering teams to own DevSecOps," Mandy Andress writes "DevSecOps can be difficult to implement because it involves a mindset shift for security teams, engineers and developers."[3] It is no wonder that asking security professionals to take a major risk in transforming the fundamental way in which they work may be met with resistance. For a transformation to be successful, you must understand the impact it will have on people and the goals and concerns of those people.

Transforming while Delivering

Like other business transformations, the DevSecOps transformation is also challenging for established companies, because you must transform while continuing to deliver with existing models of working. Security operations can never stop, so pausing existing security activities to implement new ways of working is not an option. Teams often struggle because they lack the knowledge of these new ways of working and lack the time to dedicate to learning and establishing them. Just about every security team is fully occupied with day-to-day tasks, and this sort of transformation requires additional work, which must be accommodated. You cannot stop existing monitoring or security incident response activities while you revamp them.

---

[3] Andress, Mandy. "It'S Time for Engineering Teams to Own DevSecOps." ComputerWeekly.Com. TechTarget, September 23, 2022.

Transformational Leadership

To lead transformation, you must be a transformational leader. As a leader, you must be empowering, transparent, collaborative, agile, instructive, innovating, and customer focused.

There are many studies of what it means to be a transformative leader. Jeff Dyer and Hal Gregersen did an extensive study on the topic in their book, *Innovator's DNA: Mastering the Five Skills of Disruptive Innovators*. In it they write, "We believe that a leader's ability to successfully drive innovation largely boils down to something we call *innovation capital*, a multifaceted set of characteristics that allows the leader to acquire and effectively deploy the human and financial resources required to take a risky and novel idea and turn it into an innovation with impact." They describe this as a mix of characteristics, including associating, questioning, observing, networking, and experimenting.

A separate study from *Harvard Business Review* found that innovative leaders exhibited the following 10 characteristics:

- Display excellent strategic vision
- Have a strong customer focus
- Create a climate of reciprocal trust
- Display fearless loyalty to doing what's right for the organization and the customer
- Put their faith in a culture that magnifies upward communication
- Are persuasive
- Excel at setting stretch goals
- Emphasize speed
- Are candid in their communication
- Inspire and motivate through action[4]

---

[4] Zenger, Jack, and Joseph Folkman. "Research: 10 Traits of Innovative Leaders." Harvard Business Review. December 15, 2014. https://hbr.org/2014/12/research-10-traits-of-innovative-leaders.

Different studies have produced different lists, but as the study in *Innovators DNA* showed, no one skill defines an innovative leader. There is, instead, a combination of skills and behaviors that help a leader drive innovation.

What is certain is that the world is changing, and leaders must change too in order to successfully drive the DevSecOps transformation. The role of the *chief information security officer (CISO)* has fundamentally changed over the past decade. With the increasing threat landscape and the increasing media attention to wide-scale breaches, the CISO's role has become increasingly more central to all companies. Boards of directors are paying increasingly more attention to cybersecurity and demanding higher rigor across industries.

One of the key changes in the role of the CISO is from operational manager to strategic driver. It is no longer sufficient for a CISO to keep the machinery of security running and to execute the direction of the CEO. The CISO must understand the business and make strategic business decisions, balancing security and the customer.

As technology leaders move to more strategic roles within the organization, they also must move from being a cost controller to being a value driver. More and more, you can look at security as a value to your customers. So often security is thought of only as a cost center. As the tech industry shifts its focus from delivering product and services to delivering user experiences, you need to find new ways to make security a value driver for your company. You cannot be satisfied by simply driving cost efficiency; you cannot be satisfied to simply have fewer security incidents; you must work more closely with the business to drive value for the company.

THE KEYS TO A SUCCESSFUL TRANSFORMATION

DevSecOps transformation is difficult, but there are certain steps you can take to help ensure your transformation is successful. Transformation is a journey, and not one that has a distinct destination. Any transformation will undoubtedly have obstacles and setbacks that you'll need to overcome, but as you approach your transformation, the steps in the following sections can help ensure that you get the results you desire.

Begin with the End in Mind

One of the keys to driving a successful transformation is to have a vision of where you will be at the end of the transformation. Because transformations such as DevSecOps require all people to be working toward the same goal, it is critical that the end goal be identified and clearly articulated to everyone. It is important to build a shared vision with concrete goals, objectives, and key results in a measurable format. For DevSecOps transformations, this means you must understand not just what you are doing but why you are doing it. Using an outcome-based approach and clearly measurable competencies, you can successfully drive DevSecOps in a large and diverse environment.

If you are doing DevSecOps to increase security while improving the speed of delivery to your customers, first define how you will measure the results. Typical measurements to examine include security incidents over time, number of vulnerabilities identified in production, and amount of time features take to go from the backlog to production. Additional information about metrics is available in Chapter 8. The metrics you arrive at must reflect the high-level business value that security engineers, business leaders, and customers expect. You must measure it at the start of your journey and track the progress throughout. By defining where you want to go, you create a north star to set the direction for the entire team. By measuring progress in that direction, you ensure that the changes are having the intended results and moving you in the right direction.

Start Small and Find Early Wins

Midsize to large organizations make the common mistake of trying to do DevOps for the entire organization at once in a homogeneous way. In trying to do everything at the same time, you can often fail to make any progress at all. Worse yet, you can create failures that provide the perfect excuse for detractors to block any positive change.

The best course of action is to look at ways you can start small and find early wins that can be examples for other teams to follow. In an organization that may have tens or hundreds of Agile development teams, find one or maybe two that are really innovative and want to take time to implement DevSecOps practices. If you can find those thought leaders, they can pave the way for the rest of the company.

When identifying these teams, it is best to ensure that they have a positive standing in the company and a track record of delivering. You should also ensure that they are interested in sharing information about their successes. Look for teams that are willing to do activities such as interviews, posting metrics about their successes, writing stories about their work, and sharing those stories at your company events so that they can become evangelists for your transformation. Once you have identified these teams, make sure you are investing the time and resources to set them up for success.

You can also identify quick wins by identifying pain points within your organization. These pain points are generally well known and easy to identify. One of the quickest ways to identify these pain points is simply by asking. Hold interviews with key stakeholders and engineers across the organization and ask them what their biggest cybersecurity challenges are. If you listen, you should be able to rapidly identify common themes that can be addressed to deliver impactful results quickly. For example, if you're spending millions of dollars on long, drawn-out, manual deployment cycles and you can reduce that significantly by automating the deployments, that is going to be a big win for you and your customers. These sorts of wins help build the momentum you need to drive the transformation forward.

Focus on the Cultural Transformation

Far too many transformations focus on the technology and not the cultural transformation that must accompany the new technology. You cannot buy a tool to make your transformation a success. Because this is a cultural transformation, it is important to keep in mind the impact that it will have on the people that make up the company and help deliver great products and services.

DevSecOps requires a new way of thinking. Security engineers must reorient themselves toward building systems that enable and empower others to make more secure products rather than implementing security themselves. Developers must reorient themselves to understand principles of secure coding and make security engineering part of their daily work. This type of cultural change and mindset shift requires significant work, including process reengineering and training. It is also not sufficient to simply provide one training and think everyone will just get on board. DevSecOps and the underlying DevOps principles need to be built into the ways of working so that it is reinforced through processes. Only when they are built into the ways of working, into daily work, will they really permeate the culture in a meaningful way.

DevSecOps requires a new way of thinking. Security engineers must reorient themselves toward building systems that enable and empower others to make more secure products rather than implementing security themselves. Developers must reorient themselves to understand principles of secure coding and make security engineering part of their daily work.

Measure Progress

To drive progress in any DevSecOps transformation, it is critical that you measure your progress. It is important to take a multifaceted approach to measurement, looking at every level of the transformation. There are two key aspects that must be measured, the competencies that are key to DevSecOps and the business outcomes. It is important to measure both of these to ensure you are moving forward with the DevSecOps transformation and that it is having the intended results. Additional detail on measuring transformation can be found in Chapter 8.

Transparency is a critical component of DevOps culture, and these measurements can provide a great opportunity for transparency. In addition to measuring the progress, you should make sure to share that information across your organization. *Information radiators* are informational displays that are placed in central locations to share information across the teams. These can take the form of large monitors, whiteboards, or glass walls for sticky notes. You can leverage information radiators for that data so that you can share that data among teams. Not only does this encourage teams to progress against those measurements, but it also facilitates learning. Teams that are struggling will be motivated to perform better, and teams that are performing well can serve as exemplars. Teams needing assistance can seek the help of other teams that may be performing well in the areas where help is needed. While it is good to share this information, it is important that this not become a tool that contributes to a culture of fear or retribution. It needs to be part of a collaborative and learning culture, where teams work together to drive each other to do their best.

Leverage Outside Help (As Appropriate)

External vendors and consultants can be a benefit for transformational work; however, there is a balance here as over-reliance can be detrimental to long-term transformation success. Often, it is extremely useful to have an external vendor help assess the status of a transformation and provide key recommendations. An independent third party can provide a relatively unbiased perspective and bring in experience from transformations from other companies.

It is also important to keep in mind that transformation requires work, a lot of work, and it is foolish to think that current people within an organization can simply take on this work in addition to all the work they are already doing. There is, of course, a cost factor here as well. Bringing in external resources is an expense for the organization. If you are planning on doing a transformation with existing resources, you are likely setting yourself up for failure. In addition, placing additional burden on current resources is likely to cause burnout, thus leading to increased turnover, the cost of which can far exceed the potential cost of supplementary resources. Additional resources and time must be allocated to the transformation, and often, external vendors help offset the resource requirements of this work. However, you should not be over-reliant on this sort of external help.

Ultimately, the people in the organization must understand, learn, and do the work. Internal resources must begin to adjust to new ways of working. You cannot simply hire an external vendor to "transform you." This is especially important as most transformations do not have a clear start and end. Few transformations are ever fully complete.

Especially in DevOps, there is always more that you can do, even for companies that are relatively mature in the DevSecOps practices. You need to build expertise in-house and develop internal processes to continue to drive transformation in the absence of external help. External resources must have clearly defined goals and expectations and, most importantly, a clear definition of when their job is complete. Ultimately, while external resources can help drive transformation forward, they must be balanced with internal resources and processes to drive continual learning and continual improvement.

Build a Communications Campaign

One of the most challenging and most important components of a DevSecOps transformation is winning over the hearts and minds of the stakeholders and the participants. This requires extensive communication.

When thinking through your communications plan, it is useful to think of it as a marketing campaign. You can't simply say, "Hey, everybody, do DevSecOps," and expect the company to make the drastic changes required. You need to create a consistent communication plan tailored for the audience and the many channels via which they consume information. You cannot simply communicate once in an email and think you are done. You must leverage all the communication channels, including town halls, intranets, blog sites, news updates, and timely emails, and think about ways to get people to talk about it and engage with it.

In developing the plan, you need to understand the entire scope of your implementation while focusing on short-term goals so as not to overburden the team with too much change. This plan must include the definitions of the teams involved, projected process changes in the short term, and expected realization of the short-term goals for each team.

Audience

When developing a communication plan, first identify and address the audience you are speaking to. Audiences include business-line owners who have a stake in these applications, whether the application is an internal application, such as human resources, or a revenue-producing website. It also includes technical groups that are benefiting from DevSecOps. While the data showing a decreased number of vulnerabilities may speak to security engineers, it may mean very little to a business leader.

It is important to understand each of the audiences you are speaking to, understand their concerns or focus, and craft messaging specific to them. Engineers, for example, will likely be interested in exciting new technology and innovation. Engineering managers, on the other hand, may be more interested in decreased time spent mitigating vulnerabilities found later in the development life cycle. Messaging for business leaders should focus on the value for the customer and increased revenue. At an executive level, messaging should address the stability of the company and criticality of customers and risk to long-term viability and reputation.

Communication Channels

When Coca-Cola wants to increase sales, they don't send one email message and then sit there wondering, "Why isn't everyone drinking our soda? Didn't they get our email?" They have vast marketing campaigns across every possible communication stream. They have TV campaigns, email campaigns, web campaigns, in-store marketing, and product placement in movies and TV. They work to get the message to consumers wherever their consumers are, and then they repeat that message again and again and again.

As a technologist who wants to effect positive change, you must get better at thinking like business managers and marketing executives. There is a common misconception among engineers that if they build something great, people will flock to it because, hey, there's this great tech-thingy they built and why wouldn't everyone use it? As a security engineer, you may feel that the value of security is self-evident; however, this is rarely the case with people who are not part of the security world. The reality is that unless people know about it, they cannot use it, and, even beyond that, it requires continued communication to change behavior.

Engagement with your audience should also include social media and company chat platforms. Load up these information radiators with metrics. When you have a team that is doing many deployments a day and you have them put up a dashboard showing their performance metrics and the release metrics, people can see that and then want to improve to attain that kind of performance level. This should be an ongoing marketing campaign with many different channels of information distribution and many different pieces to the message that you want to distribute.

TRANSFORMATION CHALLENGES

Just as there are several keys to driving successful transformation, there are also pitfalls to be avoided to successfully drive the DevSecOps transformation.

Cultural Inertia

While many organizations may think they want transformation, many do not realize that they need to fundamentally change their behavior and their mindset nor do they understand how difficult this can be. Inertia is the physical property wherein a body in motion tends to stay in motion, and a body at rest tends to stay at rest, unless there is a force acting on it. While this is a property of physical matter, the cultural manifestation of inertia is a powerful force that must be recognized when approaching a transformation like DevSecOps.

Often there is a person or group within an organization pushing for transformation, but the rest of the organization is not onboard. Often others will give lip service to supporting the transformation but drag their feet when it comes to actually changing. This passive resistance can kill a transformation effort. Transformations require support from the top levels of an organization as well as from the engineers and managers who will be doing the actual work to implement the changes. Although not everyone needs to be on board, it is essential that there is enough support to build momentum and carry that body in motion forward for a continued period of time.

A WILLINGNESS TO CHANGE

In addition to helping drive transformations for the companies I have worked for, I also had the privilege of running xOps, a global DevOps consulting company. During that time, we were often called upon to help companies through their transformations in DevOps, Agile, the cloud, and DevSecOps.

One large media company brought us in to help assess the status of its DevOps and provide recommendations to help drive its transformation. During the intake period, we discovered that not only weren't there development and operations teams working together but their development and quality assurance teams were siloed as well. The teams were doing development and, only when it was fully complete, handing it over to the quality assurance team in a manner much more akin to waterfal than to Agile.

Despite using Jira and Scrum to track their tickets, development of a feature was completed before it was handed off for any QA. Not only were these teams siloed, but they were working in different locations in different time zones with only a couple of hours overlap between the two. The teams were not willing to change to find ways to work together. When the leadership was approached about this fundamental misalignment, they were not interested in changing teams to increase collaboration or build a singular Agile workflow.

Although the company wanted to do DevOps, they were unwilling to make the fundamental changes needed to progress in their Agile and DevOps transformation, thus leaving little hope that their transformation would be a success.

It is useful to understand why cultural inertia may exist. Many may perceive a transformation as a risk to their job. If you are now asking all developers to integrate security into their daily work, security engineers might wonder if their job of doing security is going to be needed in the future.

In addition, it is important to understand that people have spent years of their life trying to master the current tools and processes, so changing these may be asking key resources to destroy the very thing they have dedicated years of their lives to building. Because of the deleterious effects that cultural inertia can have on the DevSecOps transformation, it is critical that you recognize it, understand its cause, and attempt to address using tools outlined in the section "Build a Communications Campaign"; this process requires empathy. Only by understanding where detractors are coming from can you begin to address their concerns.

Only by understanding where detractors are coming from can you begin to address their concerns.

Once you have a firm understanding of where the cultural inertia stems from, you must take action to address it by speaking to those concerns directly. You can help people recognize that these changes provide new opportunities by moving people to better jobs with new and exciting technology. You can also provide rewards, such as compensation and promotions for those who step up and take an active role in transformation. If others will not change, they may need to find new roles or exit the organization altogether. By understanding the concerns that drive cultural inertia, you can take concrete and measurable steps to address them.

Lack of Leadership Support

DevSecOps transformations take time, money, resources, and sustained effort. To have these things in a company of any size requires support from the top. Transformation cannot be done by will alone, and it cannot be done in your "spare time." Without the time or money to dedicate to a transformation, it is not likely to succeed. Ensuring that resources are available requires the support of top leadership.

A LOSS OF LEADERSHIP SUPPORT

At one company I worked at, we had a massive DevOps transformation underway. The transformation brought in people from all different teams, including QA, development, operations, and the business. In the middle of this transformation, the company leadership changed, and the new leadership did not see the value of DevOps. Suddenly, people from across the company were reallocated to other efforts. Without the support of executive leadership, resources for the transformation were quickly diverted, and the effort died on the vine.

One way to mitigate this threat from the start is to clearly identify both the costs of the transformation and the expected benefits. As discussed earlier, having a clear articulation of the expected results from the outset is critical. This can help offset the possibility of changing course midway through your transformation. If there is broad agreement on both the expected costs and the expected benefits of the transformation, it will significantly insulate against the possible impact of shifting priorities at a leadership level.

Lack of Contributor Buy-In

While it is important to have support from the top, it is equally, if not more important, to have support from the engineers and managers who will be doing the work of transformation. These are the people who will need to implement new tools, adopt new ways of thinking, and change the way they work on a day-to-day basis. Without their support, transformations often fail.

With contributors, it is also important to look for signs of passive resistance. Identify the people who say they are willing to change but then find reasons to delay or present roadblocks at every step. This sort of passive resistance can be even more toxic to transformation and can be an effective method of derailing progress. This type of resistance gives rise to questions about why the transformation is not progressing with answers that may be less obvious than when people are open about their reservations and concerns. Everyone is "on board," so why aren't things moving forward? These questions may spread disillusionment with the transformation as a whole, which may threaten to derail the entire effort.

This is not to say that everyone will be on board or that this is a requirement. With any transformation, it can be expected that there will be those who are eager to engage early and those who are reticent to change at every step of the process. There will always be those people who are constantly cynical about change. It is important to be empathetic and actively listen to their concerns, as they may have some valid points.

You have to understand the value of DevSecOps in great detail, up and down the line from requirements to delivery, so when you ask them to prove their point, you have the answers in your back pocket. It is important not to be dogmatic or you will get eyerolls every time "DevSecOps" is mentioned. Be public through your communications channels about what issues have been raised and address them specifically. If you stage your implementation with reasonable short-term deliverables, success can be yours.

As exemplified with Everett Rogers' bell curve shown in figure 7.1, there will be roughly 15 percent of people who adapt to changes quickly and roughly 15 percent who Rogers categorizes as "laggard," which are people who are slow to adopt to new technologies and ways

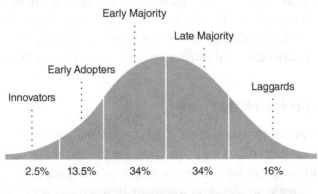

INNOVATION ADOPTION LIFE CYCLE

Figure 7.1 The innovation adoption life cycle can provide a guide for adoption rates at various stages of your DevSecOps transformation.

of working. This is okay, should be expected, and can be offset by leveraging early adopters to help move others to the DevSecOps model. However, if there are enough contributors who do not buy in, it will be challenging, if not impossible, to have a successful transformation.

Lack of Sustained Support

Lack of sustained support can also be a major problem for the DevSecOps transformation. These transformations are not short-term efforts. While there may be a significant up-front effort to get the transformation started, there will be ongoing effort to maintain the transformation and continue to learn and grow. Transformations require fundamental changes in the way people work and the tools they use. These changes can take a significant amount of time. Migrating teams to new tooling for secure code deployment alone can take anywhere from months to years. You need resources to continue to build community and lead education. You need ongoing funding for the tools and infrastructure required for DevSecOps. You cannot simply do three months of work and then wash your hands like, "All done with that transformation. Phew! Glad that's over with." Even companies with mature DevSecOps practices have opportunities to continue to refine, improve, and grow. Anyone who has been through a successful Agile transformation knows that there is always opportunity for continued improvement and that improvement requires work.

Note that this will mean sustained financial investment. The plan must include long-term financial support for the tooling, training, and people needed to continue the transformation, build a learning culture, and ensure continual learning so critical to DevSecOps.

Doing Too Much at Once

Doing too much at once can also be a surefire way to derail a transformation. Transformations are large, long-term commitments. If you try to do too much too fast, it can actually be detrimental to progress. If you try to make progress on too many items, it can mean little to no progress is made in many directions, which can be frustrating to all involved. It is important to understand the time and resources available and use those in a focused way to drive real progress on a more limited set of items.

TRANSFORMATION SPREAD TOO THIN

During one of my first DevOps transformation efforts, we were overly ambitious. We brought together representatives from development, QA, and operations and mapped out all the things we wanted to do as part of our DevOps transformation. We spun up seven work streams, each taking on a major body of work, all without any dedicated resources or funding. Week after week, we would meet to report on what the work streams had accomplished, and week after week the teams had little, if any, progress to report.

Eventually people who had started off as very motivated just stopped showing up. While everyone was doing their best and excited about the transformation, they all had full-time jobs and were stretched thin to begin with. No one wants to show up to say that they weren't able to accomplish what they had set out to do. Slowly but surely, the enthusiasm and participation dwindled.

Failure to Communicate Value

As mentioned earlier in this chapter, it is critical to understand why you and your company are undertaking the DevSecOps transformation. Not only must you understand why you are taking this on, but you must communicate that to all of the participants and the stakeholders. As discussed in the section "Build a Communications Campaign," it is important that you present that value in ways that connect to the audience you are addressing. The executive leadership and board of directors will appreciate the focus on lower risk levels for the company and faster time to market. Developers will appreciate the way in which they are empowered and the opportunity to move faster with fewer gates to deliver innovative new features to market. Security engineers will appreciate the value of building security as a shared responsibility across the organization.

Not only must you understand and communicate this value, it is also important to measure the value delivered so that you can ensure your transformation is delivering the results expected. You can explore exactly what and how to measure this in more detail in Chapter 8.

CONCLUSION

The world is transforming, and you must too. As the threat landscape continues to expand, it will take new tools and, more importantly, new ways of working. The DevSecOps transformation can help your company address these emerging challenges while continuing to be agile, adaptive, and delivery-focused to meet your customers' needs. This transformation is, at its core, a cultural transformation, which entails its own unique set of challenges. Organizations must pivot not only the tools they use to work but also how they work and adapt to new ways of thinking.

Today, technology is at the core of everything we do, and because of this, it is no longer possible to separate cybersecurity and the business. To drive transformation in this new world, you must be a leader who understands the business and customer needs. It is critical to always have a customer focus and a keen eye on the value you deliver. To do this, you must collaborate across engineering and business lines.

Successful transformations require transformational leaders and security engineers who can help lead this transformation. These newly emerging leaders must move from simply keeping things secure from an isolated silo to innovating and driving new business in collaboration with business and technology leaders across the company. The only way to succeed in transformation is to work together. Security engineers must lead the charge, integrated with their development counterparts, moving from being implementation engineers to being teachers and mentors.

DevSecOps requires a fundamentally different mindset. It requires that you move from thinking of security as a siloed organization to thinking of it as something every engineer must participate in as part of their daily work. This mindset requires openness, transparency, trust, and collaboration. Everyone who participates in the DevSecOps transformation needs to embody these characteristics.

The struggles to drive transformation will be multiplied tenfold without support from both the top and the bottom of the organization and without leaders emerging in all areas. Whatever your role in the organization, you have the opportunity to lead the DevSecOps transformation. Never has transformation been more important. Transformation and continuous improvement must be part of how you work every day.

CHAPTER 8

Measuring DevSecOps

INTRODUCTION

For a DevSecOps transformation to succeed, it is critical to measure it. To truly have a culture of continual learning, you must measure the progress. The very act of defining these measures can help ensure that you have properly articulated the direction you want to take. Tracking progress against these measures helps ensure that you are moving in the right direction and delivering the intended results.

At this point in the maturing DevSecOps movement, there is a huge variety of metrics. It is possible to look at metrics from different organizational levels, for many different purposes, and for different timescales. The metrics that the security operations team lead needs to manage their team on a daily basis will necessarily be different from the metrics that the board should review to make investment decisions on an annual basis. While there may be some overlap between audiences, you must consider the audience and the results you are trying to achieve by measuring and reporting. Ultimately, it is important that your metrics drive action for which they are designed. If the selected metrics do not provide value and drive action, they should be abandoned. Periodic review of the metrics should be performed to make sure that the evolving organizational needs are properly addressed.

Although there are a broad range of metrics that may be useful for your security program, this book focuses on metrics that are specific to DevSecOps and the DevSecOps transformation. The U.S. General Services Administration (GSA) released a relatively comprehensive list of DevSecOps metrics in its "DevSecOps Guide," which can be found at `tech.gsa.gov/guides/dev_sec_ops_guide`.

While this provides a good reference, some of these are overly broad and cover subjects outside of the scope of DevSecOps. At the same time, some metrics, such as *mean time to resolve (MTTR)*, which looks at the time it takes to resolve an incident, are not unique to DevSecOps but have sufficient overlap to be included in DevSecOps reports. This chapter focuses on metrics that are squarely within the domain of DevSecOps.

Any Metric Can Be Manipulated

It is almost always possible to manipulate a metric, and there is a potential to drive negative behavior by focusing too much on any one metric. MTTR and ticket closure rate are prime examples of this. If you myopically focus on the time it takes to close a ticket and even go as far as incentivizing (paying bonuses, etc.) based on this, people will find a way to game the system to drive down the time tickets are open. Examples include behavior such as not opening tickets until the issue is resolved so that they can open and close tickets almost instantaneously, or, perhaps less nefariously, simply rushing to get tickets closed, favoring ticket closure over other priorities such as quality and customer experience. In cases such as these, well intended metrics can create a very negative customer experience.

One way to lessen the risk of people manipulating metrics is to ensure that you use multiple metrics and avoid over-reliance on any one factor. If you are looking at MTTR, you should also look at metrics like customer satisfaction and ticket reopen rates. Another way to help ensure that people do not try to manipulate metrics is to set the right tone and develop a learning culture in which people know that the things you are measuring are being used to drive continual improvement and not as a means to micromanage or enforce. These types of metrics should not be tied directly to an individual's performance but should be looked at on a team level to drive direction. As discussed in Chapter 3, "DevSecOps People," punitive applications of measurement are likely to breed a culture of fear and mistrust.

Service level objectives (SLOs) set targets for things such as availability or delivery of services. SLOs are different than service level agreements, which are generally externally facing commitments to customers. However, they are related in that SLOs may underpin SLAs. That is, it may be necessary to achieve one or more internal targets (SLOs) to ensure external commitments (SLAs) are met.

All too often people are hesitant to commit to SLOs because they fear they will be punished if the target is not achieved. Given the number of changing parameters—such as changing market conditions, turnover, and shifting priorities—people may feel they cannot reasonably predict their ability to meet specific SLOs. One good practice to overcome this fear is to begin by acknowledging you don't have the data and make a best estimate for an SLO target. Communicate clearly that the first step is only to measure and then adjust at a later date if required based on the additional information this initial measure provides. If there is an incident that takes longer than expected to resolve, the response must not be punitive; instead, it should be approached as an opportunity for learning to understand why this happened and look for opportunities to improve going forward.

While metrics can certainly be manipulated in one direction or another, this should not be used as an excuse not to measure things. Just because it is possible to artificially alter MTTR does not mean you should not track it. By ensuring you are getting as full a picture as possible, looking from many different angles through many different metrics, and by building a learning culture, you can make metrics a powerful guiding tool for your organization.

Start Small and Iterate

Start small and iterate when approaching the development of a new metrics program. The amount of data you can collect can be overwhelming, so it is useful to start with just one or two metrics you want to measure, collect the data around them, and then add another.

Metrics will generally be wrong the first time you measure them, and that needs to be okay. Almost every time you start to track new data, the first time you share it, you will be incorrect because people have not previously paid attention to the accuracy of the data. The attention that publishing incorrect data draws will drive corrective action. Only after the metric has been published for a few months should you expect the accuracy of the data to be at a level to drive strategic action. Ultimately, starting with bad data is almost always better than waiting for perfection or not starting at all.

Metrics will generally be wrong the first time you measure them, and that needs to be okay.

STARTING WITH BAD DATA

As the leader of global technical operations teams, when I share a new metric, I am open about the fact that there will be errors in the data the first time it is presented. This data is bound to be inaccurate because no one has paid attention to it previously.

At one company when I rolled out the vulnerability program and presented cloud vulnerability data per application, people shouted about how there were false positives and how the data was incorrect. For me, this argument was actually a sign of great success. It indicated that people were now paying attention to the data. It meant that teams cared about the metrics and would take action. If they care enough to shout about it, they will care enough to begin to dig into the data and start to make sure it is accurate.

After a couple months of presenting cloud vulnerability data, the number of vulnerabilities dropped by almost 50 percent. This was, in part, because there were a lot of false positives, but it was also because there was a significant amount of low-hanging fruit that teams had not resolved because they did not have the visibility. If we had waited until the data was 100 percent accurate before presenting it, we would have waited forever because those same teams would never have taken action to resolve the underlying data issues.

As you develop your metrics program, ensure that perfection is not the enemy of progress. Many people get lost in the vast morass of potential metrics. This can be an excuse to take no action at all. Choose easy first steps and gradually increase the scope by adding additional metrics. In addition, it is often only when you see new data that you can really determine what data you want. Often the data you present raises new questions and helps you define the data you really are interested in.

KEYS TO A SUCCESSFUL METRICS PROGRAM

While metrics programs can be complex, the following are a few key elements that will help ensure that your metrics program is successful:

- **Automated**—Make sure that whatever metrics you develop are delivered in an automated way. Ideally this should be through live dashboards that can be accessed at any time. If it takes too much effort to generate the metrics you review, they are likely to be discarded when workloads increase. By presenting them on an active dashboard, you ensure that they are not only automated but always up-to-date, removing the possibility that you need an extensive process to manually generate them on a periodic basis.

- **Reproducible**—Whatever metrics you develop should be easily reproducible. This generally goes hand in hand with automation. If you are automatically generating your metrics and reporting, you can ensure that the time period is configurable. This enables you to easily regenerate metrics for prior time periods.

- **Transparent**—Share as much as you can without exposing yourself to additional security risk. The more people have visibility into the metrics, the more you will develop shared learning and shared direction.

- **Actionable**—Ideally your metrics should drive action. If you are simply reporting metrics for the sake of reporting, then you may be wasting effort. You should make sure that the data you are looking at is driving action or that if a change was observed, it would prompt action. If the metrics are not influencing behavior, you need to question whether they are really needed.

OPERATIONAL METRICS

Some of the most important DevSecOps metrics are the ones that help you drive your business on a day-to-day basis, the *operational* metrics. These are key metrics to look at daily, weekly, and monthly to determine if your DevSecOps practice is delivering the results expected.

As you develop your operational metrics, you should carefully consider the periodicity of metrics. Different metrics may be more relevant and provide more value for different periods of time. Some metrics should be reviewed on a daily basis, while others will be more useful for trending purposes on a weekly or monthly basis.

- Things like number of attacks and high-frequency incidents are good to review on a daily (or even hourly) basis, as they may represent an emergent trend or imminent threat that you need to take immediate action on.

- Other metrics, such as MTTR may make more sense to review on a weekly and/or monthly basis, as this is more indicative of longer-term trends. While these need to be acted upon, because the data is sparser, it may not fluctuate significantly on a daily basis, and looking at it more frequently may not prove valuable.

The following sections provide details on some of the most valuable metrics to adopt in your DevSecOps program.

Number of Incidents

Number of incidents is an obvious and valuable metric to review. For these purposes, you should think of an *incident* as an unplanned interruption or degradation of service. Incidents also include the failure of a system that may cause impact to service even if it has not yet done so. This would track the highest priority incidents such as breaches or DDoS attacks that bring down a service as well as lower-priority incidents such as users being locked out of their accounts or DDoS attacks that have been mitigated.

INCIDENTS BY PRIORITY OVER TIME

Incidents resolved by priority over time is one of my favorite metrics to review. It provides good insight into security as well as the workload for the team. I review this data on a weekly basis on our weekly security standup. Figure 8.1 shows the number of incidents per day broken down by priority.

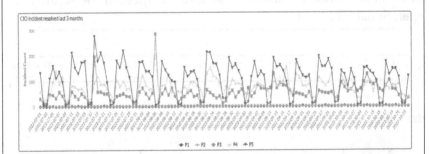

Figure 8.1   Number of incidents by priority can be a great way to ensure incidents are being prioritized correctly. This data can also identify potentially problematic spikes in incident activity.

In general, you should expect to see a higher number of lower-priority incidents. If you are not, it is worth investigating why. One team I worked with had a very low number of low-priority incidents. When I investigated, it was revealed that they were simply not tracking minor incidents. This is a common practice but quite problematic. The low-priority incidents are often the bulk of the work for the security team. You need to track these, as they provide insight into what is

(continues)

(*continued*)

driving the workload. It is also important to track low-priority incidents because, while one minor incident may not be problematic, many may lead to significant issues, what is often referred to as "death by 1000 papercuts."

Incidents by priority is generally cyclical, so you should keep an eye out for spikes or other anomalies.

Prioritizing incidents is beyond the scope of this book, but it is important to find a consistent and standard way to do this. IT service management provides a good, standardized way to prioritize incidents that will also ensure a similar prioritization method for security and operational incidents.

Lower-priority incidents generally occur significantly more frequently than high-priority incidents and therefore are drivers of trends and overall workload volume. High-priority incidents are, ideally, relatively infrequent, so they may not provide as good of a measure on a daily basis but should be trended over longer periods of time.

Note—*It may be necessary to report separately on major incident trends as the lower-priority incidents can skew the scale to such an extent that high-priority incidents become difficult to see.*

Vulnerabilities by Service Level Objective

Vulnerabilities give insight into the risk exposure your systems may have. While it is good to know the total number of vulnerabilities, this may not be that illuminating because the vulnerabilities may be of different priorities. A high-severity vulnerability obviously is much riskier to the organization than a low-severity vulnerability, so simply lumping them all together does not provide valuable information.

The *Common Vulnerability Scoring System (CVSS)* provides a good method for determining the criticality of vulnerabilities. Whether you use this or another prioritization method, you should take this method into account when tracking vulnerabilities in your system.

While looking at the total number of vulnerabilities by severity is useful, there is also an age element to vulnerabilities. As new vulnerabilities are arising every day, even the most secure systems will have some vulnerabilities. In addition, some vulnerabilities are so low risk that it may not make sense to address them. Because of this, it is important to measure how old vulnerabilities are and, more importantly, whether you are resolving them within a timeframe that is acceptable from a risk perspective for your business.

To do this, you can set SLOs, discussed earlier in the chapter, to set target timeframes by which you want to see vulnerabilities closed for the risk levels that are acceptable for your business. For example, you may say that high-severity vulnerabilities must be remediated within 24 hours, while low-severity vulnerabilities should be resolved within 5 days. You can then track the percentage of vulnerabilities resolved within the defined SLO. By doing this, you do not need to look at the number of vulnerabilities, the number of vulnerabilities by severity, or resolution time by vulnerability, because all of these are encapsulated in your SLO metric. By tracking vulnerability SLOs, you can determine if your business is within acceptable risk levels and take action if it is not.

Mean Time to x

Mean time to respond (MTTr) provides the amount of time it takes to respond to an incident, while MTTR (capital *R*) tracks how long it takes to resolve incidents. Looking at MTTR by priority helps to see the mean time it takes to resolve each incident by priority. This can be a highly valuable metric and one of the items to look at as part of a continual improvement program, as it speaks directly to whether a company is increasing the speed at which incidents are resolved. As DevSecOps practices are implemented, you should expect to see

MTTr and MTTR reduced. CI/CD, small batch deployments, automated testing, and cross-team collaboration all contribute to lowering MTTx.

It should be noted that there are some problems with mean time metrics. In an article entitled "MTTR Is a Misleading Metric—Now What?"[1] Courtney Nash lays out some of the deficiencies of MTTr, including the fact that the mean is highly impacted by outliers. She also notes that incident data is relatively sparse, which reduces the value of an average value. The article suggests that mean time to resolve or SLOs may be a better way to look at incident data. That said, mean time to resolve can provide value from a directional standpoint.

Note—*If you see a steady increase in MTTR over time, this is an indicator that something is changing that bears further investigation.*

Reliability

Reliability from a security perspective refers to how long an application or service performs effectively without a security incident. One way to measure this is by looking at mean time between failures (MTBF). MTBF calculates the average between the incident start times and provides the frequency of outage. It is calculated as follows:

MTBF = Total operational time/Number of failures

This is an important metric to trend over time, as it lets you know how long, on average, a system runs without an incident. Tracking MTBF over time provides another indicator of whether measures to increase security are effective.

BOARD-LEVEL METRICS

Although it is important to measure the effectiveness of your security posture on a daily and weekly basis by looking at security operations trends, you should also report on effectiveness of the DevSecOps

---

[1] Nash, Courtney. "MTTR Is a Misleading Metric—Now What?" Verica. November 4, 2021. www.verica.io/blog/mttr-is-a-misleading-metric-now-what.

program to senior executives and the board of directors. If the company is investing considerable time and effort on the DevSecOps transformation, it is critical to show the results of these efforts in improved security and time to market to ensure continued support.

When considering board-level metrics, you should consider what it is the board really wants to know. The board will be looking at investment in security along with other investments the business is, or could be, making. Ultimately, the board will be focused on risk exposure for the company and investment around risk. The board will want to know if you are secure or, more specifically, if the *residual risk*, that is, the risk remaining after the mitigation steps you have taken, meets the businesses risk tolerance. In addition, they will want to ensure that the investment the company is making in risk mitigation provides the most value possible.

The following sections provide some key board-level metrics to consider when developing your security metrics program.

Measuring Risk

There has been quite a lot written about measuring cybersecurity risk—in fact, there are entire books written on it. This chapter does not go into a detailed analysis of risk measurement methodologies, but what is critical to note is that, from a board-level perspective, the purpose of the cybersecurity program is mitigating risk and making business decisions about balancing risk and investment. For more detail on ways to measure risk, you can read *How to Measure Anything in Cybersecurity Risk*, by Douglas W. Hubbard, Richard Seiersen, and Stuart McClure.[2] To show the effectiveness of a DevSecOps program, it is therefore critical that you have a standard method of measuring risk so that you can show the impact of the program on the risk levels.

Ultimately, what you want to be able to say at a board level is that, based on x dollars of investment in a specified risk reduction activity,

---

[2] Hubbard, Douglas W., and Richard Seiersen. 2016. How to Measure Anything in Cybersecurity Risk. 1st ed. Wiley & Sons. https://doi.org/10.1002/97811191 62315.

you moved your company's risk level from A to B. That is, for a given investment, you were able to reduce the risk level by a measurable amount. To do this, it is important to first measure your baseline risk levels. Then you measure your risk level after mitigating controls (such as implementing a code scanning solution in your deployment pipeline) to leave you with a new risk level referred to as *residual risk*. Note that you can use this same approach to talk to potential future investment cases and to evaluate the impact of multiple different investment opportunities. If a $1 million investment in one tool yields a higher-potential risk reduction than investment in another, similarly priced tool, that analysis should be valuable input in guiding the investment decision. Over time, this should be the key to your board-level reporting. Look at the investment made and the reduction in risk levels associated with those investments.

Risk Work

Another great metric to look at for senior executive reporting is the amount of time spent mitigating risk. In *From Project to Product*, Mik Kersten introduces the concept of flow metrics, which provide a great mechanism for measuring risk-based work. *Project to Product* provides a way of measuring delivery of value in the development life cycle. He breaks work down into flow items, which are categorized into four key types: Feature, Defect, Risk, and Debt. By implementing this type of measurement through tagging of work items, it is possible to see how much work is dedicated to risk mitigation activities such as remediating vulnerabilities or meeting regulatory requirements.

There is no "right" level of risk-related work. For a new startup trying to launch a product to a friendly test market, it may be quite acceptable to limit the amount of risk-based work and focus on feature delivery. On the other hand, making a new feature for a widely available product in the healthcare space dealing with patient information may require a considerable amount of risk-based work. Explicitly calling out this type of work and measuring it against other types of work enables business leaders to make conscious decisions about the amount of work being dedicated to these and other competing types of work.

INSIGHTS FROM FLOW METRICS

When Wiley first implemented flow metrics, I noticed that most groups in the CIO organization were spending little, if any, time on risk-related work. This was quite shocking to me, as I was both the CIO and the CISO. However, it made clear that we were not focusing enough on cybersecurity. We adjusted our workloads to allow more time for risk-related activities and ensure that some risk-based work was allocated in every sprint, making sure that security was truly part of everything we did. We also set targets across the entire technology team for the amount of risk-based work that teams should be doing to ensure that everyone was making risk mitigation a priority.

Spend

Aside from resource time, cybersecurity investment is the other key item of interest from a board level. You must let the board know how much you are investing in cybersecurity and the benefits this investment is providing. However, total dollars, or even total dollars by team, does not provide the most useful view of this information. What may be more pertinent at a board level is to quantify how much you are spending on specific risk-mitigation activities. One way to do this is to look at spend against your cybersecurity framework categories. If, for example, you are using the NIST framework, you may want to look at spend for each of the NIST functions: Identify, Protect, Detect, Respond, and Recover. This can be further enhanced by looking at how you are performing against each of these categories. If you are spending the most money on Identify but scoring lowest on that function, you may want to reevaluate how you are allocating funds for that function.

Another way to break up your spend in a way that may resonate with the board is to look at spend per layer of security. Taking a Defense in Depth approach, you can show spend on application layer, host layer, network layer, data layer, and so on. Again, by breaking up spending beyond resources, infrastructure, and software, you identify what this money is going to protect. If you are not already tagging spend against these categories, it may take some effort to break up spending in this way, but it will be well worth it.

Once spend is properly analyzed, you may want to also benchmark spend against other companies. To the extent possible, you should focus on companies of a similar size in your industry. The goal is not necessarily to spend less than these other companies but, rather, to use these benchmarks to make strategic decisions. You may very well decide that you want security to be a strategic advantage and therefore make a conscious decision to invest more than your competition. These benchmarks may also lead to important realizations about spending. If you find you are spending significantly more than competitors, investigation may reveal opportunities where you could be reducing spend without compromising security. Alternatively, this analysis may offer opportunities from a marketing perspective, as you can let your customers know that you are taking their security seriously and investing more heavily than your competition.

Detected Intrusion Attempts

All too often, organizations do not think about cybersecurity until a breach has occurred. In the article "7 key cybersecurity metrics for the board and how to present them," Andrew Froehlich says, "Give the board a picture of the overall number of threats the business faces at any given time." Information about detected intrusion attempts or blocked phishing attempts can be quite useful in highlighting the persistent threat to the organization as well as the positive impact current investment is having.

It's important to strike a balance here, because reporting too many threats and metrics can begin to feel too low level and operational for a board-level view, but it is also important to paint a picture of the ongoing threat that your company faces. The correct amount of attack metrics you provide depends on the knowledge of your board and their interest in this sort of information. That said, it is important to paint a picture of the very real and persistent attack your company is under. These metrics speak to the ongoing types of attacks that the company is subject to every day. This data also provides insight into the value the tools and security operations personnel are providing. Without this sort of information, security operations will seem like simply a cost overhead.

Attack Surface

In addition to knowing the number of intrusion attempts, it is useful to help the board understand the scope of the attack surface that you are protecting. The attack surface can include things such as the number of users, number of assets, payment processing environments, point-of-sale (POS) devices, amount of data, and number of applications and services. This information should be tracked over time, as it is likely to be correlated to security spend. For example, as the number of users increases, so too will your expense on endpoint management. This data also serves to increase the knowledge about what the key points of risk are for the business.

Performance vs. Peers

Your security posture compared to your peers is another good metric to provide at a board level. In the *TechTarget* article "7 key cybersecurity metrics for the board and how to present them," Andrew Froehlich states, "One of the best ways to showcase your cybersecurity efforts is to demonstrate how you stack up against your peers in the industry."[3] Services such as UpGuard and BitSight can provide an external security assessment of your customer-facing services and provide an overall security score. Even more importantly for board-level reports, these services can provide your competitors' scores. This is useful benchmarking data for your board to evaluate not only your security posture but also where you stand in comparison to the competition. These are also valuable points of data, as this data is also used by insurance companies as well as potential customers to evaluate the security of your services.

---

[3] Froehlich, Andrew. "7 Key Cybersecurity Metrics for the Board and how to Present Them." TechTarget. August 1, 2022.

While external security assessments provide a useful benchmark against competitors, these services only provide an external view of your security posture. They do not provide data about internal tools, processes, or teams. When you present to the board, call out that this is only one point of data about the company's security posture.

MEASURING TRANSFORMATION

If you are undertaking the DevSecOps transformation, it is important to measure your transformation to ensure that you are making progress and that it is yielding the expected results. As mentioned in Chapter 7, "Driving Transformation in Enterprise Environments," measuring your progress is one of the keys to ensuring a successful transformation. One way to think of this journey is as an experiment. The hypothesis is that by changing people, process, and technology, you will yield specified business results. To determine if the experiment is a success, you must measure both the things you are changing and the results. There are therefore two parts of what you want to measure—the end goal and the DevSecOps competencies.

Transformational Results

In measuring your transformation, it is important to go back to the concept introduced in Chapter 7, of beginning with the end in mind, that is, understanding why and then translating this into measurable goals. This book has talked about DevSecOps as driving increased security while driving a quicker time to market. With this as a starting point, you can look at ways to measure both time to market and security. Some of the key metrics in these areas include the following:

Time to market

- **Velocity**—This measures the number of items completed over a defined period of time.

- **Lead time**—This measures the time from idea creation to delivery to the customer. This includes time in the backlog.

Security

- **Risk exposure by NIST function**—This measures the risk level for each of the functions defined by NIST: Identify, Protect, Detect, Respond, and Recover.

- **Mean time to resolve (MTTR)**—As discussed earlier in this chapter, this is the time from when an incident starts until it is fully resolved.

In measuring outcomes, you should not lose sight of the human element. Highly engaged teams are reflective of the transparent and engaged culture that is core to DevOps. To measure this, you should ensure you also look at people metrics such as employee engagement as a measure of employee satisfaction. This is often measured based on periodic employee surveys.

These metrics provide a base for the type of information you are likely driving toward as a reason for your DevSecOps transformation. This is not a definitive or exhaustive list. While there are many other ways to measure security, time to market, and employee engagement, it is important to keep your target list as tightly focused as possible to set a clear target. Each organization may have its own key goals, but these are the types of data you should look at to determine if your transformation is delivering the expected results.

Transformational Competencies

Of course, you must not only measure the results; you must also track and influence the DevSecOps capabilities that you want to implement. To do this, you can leverage the classic triad of people, process, and technology and understand the key goals in each of these areas. For example, you might look at metrics for each of the following:

People

- **Ownership and accountability**—To what extent do people in the organization take accountability and ownership for their work product, deliverables, and mistakes?

- **Collaboration**—How much do people work across organizational boundaries?

- **Empowering**—To what extent do people have the tools and resources they need to do their jobs? How easy is it to get support?

- **Learning culture**—Does the organization learn from its mistakes? To what extent are learning rituals built into standard activities?

Process

- **Automated**—To what extent are automatable tasks automated? How much time is spent on daily toil?

- **Collaboration**—To what extent is cross-team collaboration built into the organizational processes?

- **Continuous improvement**—To what extent is continuous improvement built into standard processes? Do processes like postmortems and retrospectives exist?

- **Light weight**—How burdensome is process overhead? Are processes automated when they can be?

- **Measured**—To what extent are the results of processes measured?

- **Transparent**—How much visibility do people have into the organization's processes? (This would apply to everything from work requests to goals and objectives.)

- **Trustful**—To what extent do processes assume best intent?

Technology

- **SAST**—To what extent is static application security testing (SAST) used?

- **DAST**—To what extent is dynamic application security testing (DAST) used?

- **SCA**—To what extent is software composition analysis (SCA) used?

- **CI/CD integration**—What percentage of the application landscape is deployed via continuous integration and continuous deployment (CI/CD) pipelines? How mature are the organization's CI/CD pipelines?

- **IAC**—To what extent is infrastructure as code (IaC) used?

- **PAM**—To what extent is privileged access management (PAM) used?

- **Observability**—What level of visibility do teams have into their system's performance?

- **Secrets management**—To what extent are secrets properly managed within the application landscape? To what extent are secrets management tools used?

Some of these measures may be more subjective than others. For these items, surveys or descriptions of maturity levels may suffice. For example, cultural norms like "collaboration" may be hard to measure but can be included in regular surveys. Other items, such as "source code analysis," should be easier to quantify so you can determine if a tool is in place and across what percentage of your landscape.

This list is not meant to be comprehensive but should provide a good starting point. The critical elements of your DevSecOps transformation may vary. However, by defining the competencies that matter most at the beginning of your transformation, you define the specific outcomes you hope to achieve.

CAPABILITY MODELS

Capability models measure the competency within specified areas of a practice such as DevSecOps. Capability models are a useful way to evaluate process adoption to tell you where you are strong and where you have gaps. They may also help to provide insight into where you should invest to drive improvement.

DevSecOps assessments can be a key tool in this process. These frequently come in the form of surveys based on defined DevSecOps capabilities. Many vendors now offer DevOps and DevSecOps capability assessments. In addition, there are tools available with prepackaged assessments as well as tools that allow you to build your own. Use an assessment tool that has an agreed upon set of capabilities that are key to DevSecOps for your organization to measure those capabilities on a periodic basis. Assessments can help identify points of frustration for your team as well as key targets for automation. They can also help identify places where there is excess spend and opportunities for great efficiencies.

Capability models differ from maturity models. *Maturity models* measure the maturity of a tool, activity, or set of characteristics based on a linearly progressing and predefined set of maturity standards. Capability models, on the other hand, generally focus on supporting capabilities and their impact on the expected outcomes. While both can provide value, there can be some drawbacks to maturity models. In *Accelerate*, Forsgren, Humble, and Kim state that "[t]he key to successful change is measuring and understanding the right things with a focus on capabilities—not on maturity."[4] They note that maturity models tend to take a linear approach instead of a continuous learning approach. In addition, they tend to take a very static and standardized approach that may not be flexible enough for today's dynamic DevOps environment.

Today there is no universally accepted DevSecOps maturity or capability model. The Open Worldwide Application Security Project (OWASP) has released the DevSecOps Maturity Model (SDOMM),[5] and consulting companies are coming up with new models every day. Traditional cybersecurity frameworks such as NIST, ISO, and SOC2 do provide good models for evaluation but tend to omit key DevSecOps capabilities.

---

[4] Forsgren, Nicole, Jez Humble, and Gene Kim. 2018. Accelerate: The Science of Lean Software and DevOps: Building and Scaling High Performing Technology Organizations. 1st ed. Oregon: IT Revolution Press.

[5] "OWASP Devsecops Maturity Model." OWASP. Accessed May 6, 2023. https://owasp.org/www-project-devsecops-maturity-model.

While these focus on the traditional security measures, they should certainly benefit from DevSecOps. For example, the Detect component of the NIST framework will certainly see an improved rating as you implement advanced observability, which is a critical component of DevSecOps. In addition, there are several DevOps maturity models and assessments—including the DevOps Research and Assessment (DORA)—that have become standards in the DevOps community. However, to really drive DevSecOps, it is best to use something specifically focused on DevSecOps or develop your own.

If external support is required, you can leverage external vendors or help develop your own based on the capability measures mentioned here. What is important is that you develop and track your progress in a consistent manner by defining key capabilities and maturity levels appropriate for your organization. It is important that you leverage the same reporting method year after year so that you can see where you are improving and where you need to focus. Whatever model you use, you must ensure it does not become a one-time document that sits on a shelf without driving action.

It is important that you leverage the same reporting method year after year so that you can see where you are improving and where you need to focus.

There are several ways to assess progress against a set of capabilities needed for the organization. Survey-based assessments, team-based assessments, interview-based assessments, and data-based analysis provide details about the capabilities you are trying to develop. Each one of these provides valuable insight in their own right. Survey-based assessments can be sent to all technical employees to get their opinion on where the organization stands. For example, you send a survey with questions like the following:

Do you have SAST integrated into your deployment pipeline:

No.

One or two.

About half.

Yes, on most.

All deployments have SAST and do not go to production unless remediation requirements are met.

Note: *Survey design is an art unto itself. All too many surveys are poorly designed, leaving survey respondents feeling frustrated and like their time has been wasted. If you are going to develop a survey, it is best to consult someone who has expertise in this area or rely on an out-of-the-box solution. It is also important to make sure you share the results and the outcomes of the survey. Otherwise, respondents will feel like their time was not well spent.*

Although surveys can be great ways of gathering information, they are somewhat subjective in that they are based on the survey respondent's opinion and knowledge about how well a team is doing. While the subjective nature can be problematic, the opinions of your people are important. In addition, these types of surveys can provide insight into items that you may not be able to assess through more quantitative data. Competencies like collaboration and learning culture can be difficult to assess through quantitative methods and might be better suited to a survey-based approach.

This same approach can be leveraged using team leads to provide feedback on the maturity levels. Rather than sending out a survey to all technical team members, it is possible to have the team leads self-assess on the capabilities defined on the maturity model. This approach empowers team leads; however, it requires a trust-based approach that clearly emphasizes the results will not be used in a punitive manner but rather used to drive learning and continual improvement. In addition, this approach has the benefit that the evaluators are often closest to the competencies. However, this approach may exclude some vital sources of information. It may not include critical people, and it may be prone to bias for team leads who overstate their strengths.

The target of capability models and maturity models is rarely to get all teams or products to the highest rating. The investment would likely outweigh the benefits of this type of approach. In addition, the targets will be highly variable based on the maturity of the product and the goals of the organization. If, for example, a product is toward the later stages of its life and set to be deprecated in the near future, with limited changes or updates planned, it may not make sense to take the time and effort to integrate all the security tools into a CI/CD pipeline. In this case, it may be completely acceptable to run the product at its current maturity level until it is retired. Capability and maturity scores must not become punitive measures that factor into performance reviews, compensation, or advancement considerations. If these types of assessments are used to measure performance or drive disciplinary action against employees, you will develop a culture of fear. If people fear that their income or jobs may be impacted by assessment results, they may not help or, alternatively, they may provide false results. While it is important to drive improvement, this data should be taken as an opportunity to learn and grow and to build a learning culture and a system of continual learning.

COMBINE MULTIPLE MEASUREMENT APPROACHES

Wiley takes multiple measuring approaches to measure its DevOps maturity. It takes general surveys as well as assessments on the same characteristics from the team leads. This provides multiple views of the team's capabilities. By and large, what Wiley discovered was that these two methods tend to corroborate each other, which is encouraging. It indicates that the team leads as well as the larger technical population tend to have the same view on strength and weaknesses. The places where the two approaches did not corroborate provided a learning opportunity to investigate the disparity.

An interview-based approach to assessments can also provide very useful insight that may not be evident from a survey. While these are time-consuming and subjective, they tend to be highly productive in the information they uncover. Simple questions such as "What is your biggest challenge?" can uncover surprising results and great targets for improvement that might not be uncovered in a general survey on maturity of capabilities. By providing opportunities for interactive discussions and opportunities to dive deeper into participants, response interviews open up insights that surveys may not.

RESULTS FROM STAKEHOLDER INTERVIEWS

When working on a DevOps transformation for a major media company, I performed an initial assessment using DORA metrics in conjunction with in-person interviews. It was very interesting to see the similarities, and the differences, that came out of the two vantage points. Some great insight was gleaned from the interviews that did not appear in the survey, such as the fact that Dev and QA teams were spread out across time zones and, while they claimed to be using Agile, they were waiting until features were fully complete to throw the completed products over the wall to a QA team in a very waterfall-like manner.

In addition, interviews showed that communication was a major problem. More than 60 percent of interviewees mentioned communication as a core problem. While respondents indicated several different issues under the umbrella term *communication*, it was clearly one of the biggest themes. One of the primary issues identified as a communication issue was the lack of understanding of broader direction, goals, or vision. Several people felt they did not know what to focus on or how to behave, as they had no knowledge of the overall strategic direction. Other communication challenges included lack of communication between teams and lack of commitment from team members and leadership.

One simple step coming out of this assessment was to improve communication from the leadership. We ensured that there was regular communication to the team—including all-hands meetings, emails, newsletters, and the like. These were all great, low-cost opportunities to share progress, build a common vision, and articulate common goals.

In addition to assessments, it is possible to make data-based evaluations of many of the capabilities you are trying to implement. This may draw from several of the measurements discussed earlier in the chapter. By looking at the hard data, you can get objective measures of how your organization is performing. For example, you can look at the amount of time it takes to resolve major incidents by examining data directly from your incident tracking system. These metrics can also be used as comparisons against the more subjective data collected via surveys. This could be done by comparing questions about how quickly people perceive it takes for security incidents to get resolved against the data tracked in your incident management system.

Conclusion

Measuring DevSecOps transformation and delivery helps you make great strides in securing your systems through DevSecOps principles. Measuring the outcomes as well as the improvement in competencies targeted by the DevSecOps transformation not only helps measure progress but also lays the foundation for continued improvement by codifying the results you aim to achieve in a quantitative way. By looking not only at the capabilities you are attempting to implement but also at the outcomes, you can correlate the results with your action to ensure that they are having the desired results for the business. This process helps to bear out the book's thesis—if you collaborate closely and if you implement the DevSecOps principles, everyone can deliver at speed without sacrificing security.

Along the journey, you must also make sure to quantify operational metrics for the security team as well as the many stakeholders. You must understand the metrics that are useful to look at on different cadences: what is useful for the security team to look at on a daily, weekly, and monthly basis and, conversely, what data should the board review on a quarterly or annual basis. In all cases, what is critical is that the data provided helps determine if you are headed in the right direction and that the metrics developed and reviewed help you make actionable decisions to deliver the best business outcomes.

CHAPTER 9

Conclusion

INTRODUCTION

While DevOps has been around for some time now and is reaching maturity in many organizations, DevSecOps is still in its infancy. Companies that are able to bring DevOps principles to cybersecurity will reap the benefits seen from DevOps and have the opportunity to leapfrog their competition. By implementing DevSecOps, companies have the opportunity to deliver at speed without sacrificing security.

Of course, implementing DevSecOps is easier said than done. DevSecOps requires that people fundamentally change how they approach security. DevSecOps requires that they change how they work and what they do on a day-to-day basis. Security practitioners must move from implementing security to implementing security platforms; they must move from an enforcer of security gates to an advocate of security best practices. But, if you, as a security practitioner, are along for that journey and are ready to transform, the benefits that you can provide to your company are tremendous. Not only will your company benefit, but by leveraging these practices, you will propel your career forward.

PEOPLE, PROCESS, AND TECHNOLOGY

DevSecOps affects all elements of how people work, from the tools they use to the roles they take on. To truly do DevSecOps, you must change all the elements of your business from people to process to technology.

People must fundamentally change how they work to build collaboration across all teams and aspects of technical delivery. The work they do and the roles they have change. No longer is the role of security to work in an isolated silo, maintaining and monitoring the gates to prevent risk. Rather, security practitioners must build the roads to enable developers to move at the speed of business while operating in a secure environment. Security teams must move from rule enforcement to education and advocacy. At the same time, people building infrastructure and applications must take on more responsibility for security. Taking ownership for the delivery of the applications and infrastructure that's being developed for customers means taking responsibility for nonfunctional requirements such as stability, maintainability, and, of course, security.

This change in culture is one of the most difficult parts of the DevSecOps transformation, and it should not be underestimated. Building a culture of shared responsibilities and breaking down traditional silos requires a fundamental shift in mindset. You must look for ways to build this new culture of collaboration and continual learning and shift how you work together.

To support this transformation, the processes you rely on must fundamentally change as well. You need to look for ways to build DevOps principles of flow, fast feedback, and continual learning into processes such as incident management and change management. You must look to other processes that build collaboration and reinforce the shared responsibility model. Processes like tabletop exercises and red team/blue team/purple team drills create the opportunity for teams to practice the skills required for collaboration and to build these muscles so they are strong when emergencies do arise.

The core DevSecOps principles can be enabled by the tools you use. The tools help you deliver on these principles, but they do not, in and of themselves, make you DevSecOps. The CI/CD pipeline is critical to small-batch delivery, which enables experimentation, but it can also be used to push out legacy, tightly coupled code. By focusing on CI/CD and small-batch delivery, you can build the tools of security and compliance regulations directly into the means of delivering products to your customers, thereby shifting security left in the development life cycle. By focusing on automation, you can free your security engineers from the manual toil of day-to-day activities and allow them to focus on higher-value tasks, such as improving security tools, improving pipelines, and, ultimately, improving security for your customers.

Changing technology also requires changing leadership styles. As technology evolves, so too must your leadership style. As commerce has evolved from the world assembly lines to just-in-time inventory management, companies must evolve their leadership from command and control to enablement and empowerment. The move to rapid-change, small-batch deployments enables a learning culture and empowers leaders who are learning champions. The centrality of cybersecurity in just about every business means that leadership must move from being a cost controller to an innovative engine. Security leaders and practitioners must shift their focus from internal systems to external customers. We must all shift from operational managers to transformational leaders.

It is only when you look at all aspects of software delivery—the people, process, and technology—that you can really do DevSecOps. Tools alone will not make you DevOps, nor will a few SREs or a tabletop exercise. You must practice all of these and more to truly progress on your DevSecOps journey.

COLLABORATION IS AT THE CORE

If there is one thing that you take away from this book, I hope it is that you can produce better software, more quickly, and more securely through collaboration. One of the reasons I love DevSecOps is this focus on collaboration. Ultimately, what this means is that, by working together better, people can do better work. That is, if you focus on improving how you work with others, you can deliver more value to your customers. This is amazing because it means that, as a DevSecOps practitioner, you get to focus on building relationships, improving communication, and getting people to work together better. Now that's a gratifying thing to do every day, and to get to do it and deliver better business results is simply amazing.

Despite the progress made in this regard through DevOps, many organizations have not extended this philosophy to security. Security remains a siloed team in many organizations working in a secretive and siloed manner. In many ways, this is the nature of the work and the people in this line of work. If there is a security flaw, it is common that they do not go shouting about it lest others exploit it or the company lose customers and market share. Yet, time and time again, it is openness about security vulnerabilities, sharing of information, and working together that actually makes companies more secure.

If you are a security practitioner undertaking the DevSecOps journey, it is important to note that one of the things that may have to change is *you*. It is a journey of transformation of organization and organization members (you and me). You must all take on new roles. You must shift from gatekeeper to enabler, from rule maker to educator. To truly embrace openness and collaboration, you need to exemplify these traits as engineers and leaders. This may require a personal change as well because you cannot effectively be part of the change—you cannot effectively lead the change—if you are not willing to change as well.

If you are a security practitioner undertaking the DevSecOps journey, it is important to note that one of the things that may have to change is you.

MAKING SECURITY PART OF HOW YOU WORK

As you increase collaboration around security, you'll begin to integrate it into everyone's job and everything they do. This is a natural extension of the collaborative nature of DevSecOps. It is no longer an isolated security team's responsibility to ensure that the enterprise is secure. This book has, for a long time, talked about the full-stack developer and the *T-shaped employee*, which is an employee who has depth of experience in one area, such as Java programming, and also breadth of experience to understand the systems on which they run. DevSecOps emphasizes that this breadth of knowledge extends to security as well. Developers must understand secure development practices to ensure that they do not inadvertently write code that's vulnerable to attacks. Platform engineers must understand security to ensure that the platforms they are building and the APIs they are developing to interface with them are not open to attack.

With DevSecOps, security is not an afterthought. Security must be a fundamental part of everything you do. Security was previously tested at the end of the development life cycle. This was a losing proposition even when companies were only releasing twice a year. With teams releasing tens and hundreds of times a day, you must start with security in mind. You must shift security left in the development pipeline through IDEs and deployment pipelines to ensure that code is secure from the outset.

This means that security cannot be a toll gate that prevents you from going forward unless certain fees are paid. By shifting security left and developing a shared responsibility model, you make security part of everything you do. Security is simply how employees work and not something that needs to be checked or added as an afterthought. You must not build gates; instead, you should provide guardrails to allow teams to move faster and more securely.

You must not build gates; instead, you should provide guardrails to allow teams to move faster and more securely.

WHERE TO START

The DevSecOps transformation is a large one. It is a transformation journey that may last for many years. It can be difficult to determine the first steps to take, and yet those are the most critical steps. Without the first steps, you will never get anywhere.

In thinking about where to start, you can refer to two of the key suggestions for driving transformation from Chapter 7, "Driving Transformation in Enterprise Environments,"—begin with the end in mind and start small.

Begin with the End in Mind

One of the first steps to take is to determine why you want to go through the DevSecOps transformation and determine how you will measure success. This is a relatively straightforward issue that you should be able to accomplish without new tooling or significant time investment and one that will yield benefits throughout the transformation.

You should use this as an opportunity to engage stakeholders as well. While it is certainly possible to determine this by yourself, it represents a real opportunity to begin to set the tone of collaboration between your business, security, and technology teams. There is, of course, a balance here, because this is a cultural change that, by its nature takes time; you should not take undue time or measures to get buy-in from folks who may be adverse to the change from the start. However, by getting buy-in to your goals and how you are measuring them, you can help ensure that the team is aligned and take your first steps toward breaking down cultural silos.

It is also important to be cautious of the "perfect" data trap. People will often complain, "We can't use that metric, because we don't have reliable data" or "We only have that data for a subset of the population, so we can't use it" or "That data is not good." While these are all valid concerns, data becomes good only when you start to use it. You should be completely content to find a subset of data or data that may not have 100 percent accuracy because, in using the data, you help drive greater accuracy.

THE PERFECT DATA TRAP

There will be arguments when the data is first presented, such as "That data is incorrect," but I have found that those arguments are the first step toward getting accurate data. Once those arguments begin, you know you are headed in the right direction, because people have a stake in the game and are passionate about fixing it. That means they will begin to ensure the data quality improves.

On one metrics project I witnessed, the implementation first focused on collecting the data, and then they started measuring the data accuracy. There was little improvement in either the data quality or the items that were being measured. When the team asked me why things weren't improving, I asked them how they were using the metrics—a lightbulb went off. They were measuring metrics (and the accuracy of those metrics)

(continues)

(continued)

and doing nothing with them except for reviewing them with the small group that had designed and implemented the metrics program. It was only when they started reviewing the metrics with the larger team and holding the teams accountable for presenting the metrics that we began to see improvement in the accuracy as well as the business value the metrics were trying to measure in the first place.

Understanding your target state and knowing how to measure progress is an important first step, because it represents the north star toward which everyone will orient themselves. If you create a mandate without this north star, everyone may take action, but that action will be unfocused and may push and pull in many directions, thereby limiting progress and creating fiction rather than creating momentum. By taking this first step, you align everyone in the same direction. When everyone is pointing in the same direction, the results can be amazing (see Figure 9.1).

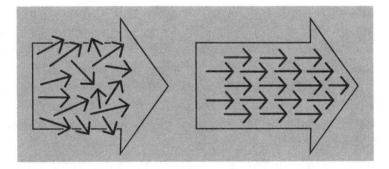

Figure 9.1   By setting measurable targets, you can align the direction in which independent groups are working to drive better results.

Start Small and Find Early Wins

The Chinese philosopher Lao Tzu said, "The journey of a thousand miles begins with one step." Keep this in mind as you begin your journey. The contrapositive is also true—if you do not take the first step, you are sure to go nowhere. What is essential is that you take a step forward and not be paralyzed by the options or the size of the undertaking.

As mentioned in Chapter 7, finding one team that can act as an exemplar team for the rest of the organization can be much more effective than trying to move the whole organization. If you are a developer who is passionate about security, perhaps this is your team. If you can find a team that is truly excited to take the DevSecOps journey and that is passionate about technology and security, you can develop a use case that is sure to provide inspiration for others. There will also be failures, but with a passionate and engaged team, those failures can be an opportunity for learning that you can bring to the rest of the organization as you continue to broaden the transformation.

Proof-of-concept pipelines can also be a good first step. These example pipelines allow you to integrate your security tools and demonstrate how successful automation works. In a similar way to exemplar teams, these provide an example that others can be inspired by and that others can use as a template.

The DevSecOps transformation is large and impacts everything you do—from people to process to technology—and it is important to address all the elements. However, if you try to take on too much, you may see significant progress in nothing. It is also such a vast undertaking that it is simple to be stuck in analysis paralysis, evaluating all options but taking no action. So, take your first step, whatever that may be, and you will be on the way to your DevSecOps transformation.

THE FUTURE OF DEVSECOPS

While some companies are just getting started, others are well along their journey in the DevSecOps transformation. Wherever you are, one thing is certain: the threat landscape and DevSecOps will continue to evolve. The changes you can see in DevSecOps are reflective of the changing technology and the sorts of shifts we are seeing in how organizations are applying technology.

Artificial Intelligence

Artificial Intelligence (AI) has emerged as one of the most dominant and transformative changes in the technology landscape. AI, the ability for machines to perceive and synthesize information and come up with novel answers, is reshaping the face of technology. It has far-reaching impacts across almost every aspect of technology, and we are already seeing the impacts on cybersecurity.

Some of the applications of AI to the threat landscape are relatively simple, such as the use to craft better phishing emails. The increasing availability of *large language models (LLMs)*, which can generate text on request, allows attacks to more easily craft messages that are used to phish for credentials. These also enable people to craft more natural sounding messages in languages that may not be their first language, expanding the ease with which people from around the world can launch attacks against targets in other countries. LLMs are also becoming increasingly efficient at impersonation. By examining public bodies of information such as speeches, AIs can quickly write messages in the tone of another person, thereby allowing attackers to more easily and accurately impersonate CEOs and CFOs to convince employees to take action. These LLMs can also be used to hold full conversations, allowing for threat actors to automate phishing campaigns beyond the initial attacks and potentially allowing them to significantly increase the number of attacks through automation.

There are also more advanced applications of AI such as *polymorphic malware attacks*. These attacks rely on AI to continuously modify malware so that the signature of a given malware is constantly changing. Because the malware is constantly changing, traditional antivirus programs do not have a set pattern that can be detected.

To respond to these rapidly developing threats, you need to rely on AI-based solutions. To detect polymorphic malware and advanced phishing attacks, you need tools that can learn and adapt to new patterns. DevSecOps lays the groundwork for organizations to be able to rapidly adapt to a changing threat landscape and add new tools to respond. If you have properly developed your deployment pipelines, you can rapidly insert new security capabilities into these pipelines. Beyond the tooling, developing a learning culture is important, as people within these organizations need to rapidly learn about AI and the new threats it poses.

Experience Management

With the shift to a product focus comes a focus on the wholistic experience of the customer. Across many industries, we are increasingly seeing this shift from the goods received to the experience involved in receiving those goods. This focus can be seen in everything from the packaging your goods come in when you order something online from Nike to the way the Starbucks barista addresses you when you buy a grande latte at your local coffee shop. Each of these is specifically tailored to build a comprehensive experience with the brand. It is not just about the coffee you buy; it is about the wholistic experience in buying that coffee. This experience builds a relationship with that brand and makes you want to keep coming back.

Security professionals need to begin thinking about overall experience as well. This means that when thinking about implementing security tools, you must consider the user experience. The tools must fit frictionlessly into the engineer's workflows. In addition, tools must be fit for purpose, addressing the function but also tailored for the group of users who will interface with them. However security fits into your organization, you must begin to think of it as a part of the overall experience of your customers, both internal and external.

Product Thinking

Increasingly you must think about security offerings as a product that is part of a wholistic experience for your users. This shift applies equally to internal tools and services as to external services. Security leaders must shift their thinking from which projects need to be done in a given year to what their capabilities are that their security services deliver to end users and customers.

Product-oriented thinking focuses more on the value delivered to the customer and less on the thing delivered within a fixed scope project. Mik Kersten discusses this change in focus in his book *Project to Product*, where he writes, "Product-oriented management focuses on measuring the results of each unit of investment that brings value to the business. Those units are products; they deliver value to a customer, and as such, the measurement must be based on those business outcomes. Funding of new value streams is based on a business case for that product, as is ongoing investment in those value streams."[1]

In the security space, you must think about security as a product that you are delivering for your customers. You must think about the value that the product delivers, the key gaps in the product, and the most valuable features that your customers need. In shifting the focus to a product-based mindset, you can bring greater focus on the customers as well as on the values that the work delivers. In addition, security leaders and practitioners should think about new security offerings that should be brought forward. Companies can add products and services such as security trainings for their customers as well as value add offerings within existing product lines. With a product-based approach, security moves from being a cost center to a value driver.

CONCLUSION

I hope this book has provided you with some insight into the people, process, and technology of DevSecOps and some help to begin your journey.

DevSecOps is a rapidly developing field, but there are many sources available to help you on the journey. You can find additional information in the following resources:

- Gene Kim; Jez Humble; et al. *The DevOps Handbook*. IT Revolution Press. (PART VI—The Technical Practices Of Integrating Information Security, Change Management, And Compliance.)

- Forsgren PhD, Nicole; Jez Humble; Gene Kim. *Accelerate*. IT Revolution Press. Kindle Edition. (Integrating Infosec Into The Delivery Lifecycle.)

---

[1] Kersten, Mik. 2018. Project to Product: How to Survive and Thrive in the Age of Digital Disruption with the Flow Framework. 1st ed. Portland: IT Revolution Press Next.

- Helen Beal; Jason Cox; et al. *Investments Unlimited: A Novel About DevOps, Security, Audit Compliance, and Thriving in the Digital Age*. IT Revolution Press.

- Kelly Shortridge and Aaron Rinehart. *Security Chaos Engineering: Sustaining Resilience in Software and Systems*. O'Reilly Media.

- Gene Kim; Kevin Behr, et al. *The Phoenix Project*. IT Revolution Press.

- Gene Kim. *The Unicorn Project*. IT Revolution Press.

- Sidney Dekker. *Understanding Human Error*. CRC Press.

DevSecOps is an exciting step in the evolution of cybersecurity. By building better collaboration across teams and by making security a shared responsibility, you can bring more secure products to market without sacrificing speed. Whether you are a security leader or just beginning your career, you can be part of the DevSecOps revolution!

ACKNOWLEDGMENTS

There have been so many people who have helped make this book a reality. Without them you would not be reading this book today.

I would like to thank my family and friends for their ongoing support and for putting up with me through it all. Special thanks to my wife, Judith, for her patience and a willingness to always listen when I needed to talk through ideas. Thanks to my father, Jon, and to my stepmother, Annie, for their unwavering support.

I had the opportunity to speak with many of the top minds in DevOps and DevSecOps space as well as some brilliant authors in the development of this book and learned so much from them! I hope some of that has translated into the knowledge I have imparted in this book. Thanks to David Seidl for all of his input on the authoring process. Thanks to Matt Titmus for his ongoing leadership of the DevOps community here in NYC and his input on the writing process. Thanks to Brian Scott, Bill Bensing, Lisa Tarsi, and Barak Brudo for their input into governance, risk, and compliance. Thanks to Aaron Rinehard for his insight into security chaos engineering. Thanks to Tapabrata "Topo" Pal for sharing his wealth of experience with DevSecOps in highly-regulated enterprise environments.

Thanks to Tom Zarb for his insight into cybersecurity and for helping to catch all of my mistakes. Thanks to Fedor Terlov and David Thatcher for reading some of the first drafts of this book and for helping build an amazing DevOps culture at Wiley.

I would like to thank the team at Wiley who helped develop our DevSecOps pipeline, including Chase Martin, Tom Zarb, Lisa Tarsi, Fedor Terlov, and Anatolii Leskovets. I learned a ton from working with this group. From governance to site reliability engineering to security, this was a great example of the type of cross-functional team that exemplifies many of the concepts highlighted in this book.

Special thanks to everyone who helped edit this book. As my acquisition editor said to me, "Writing is editing," it could not be more true, and I could not have done it without a ton of help. Thanks to Greg Fletcher for all of his tireless editing assistance. His feedback and input on every chapter of the book helped make it 10 times better than it would have otherwise been. Thanks to Jim Minatel, acquisition editor, who helped me understand the process of being an author. Thanks to Kezia Endsley for her amazing editing assistance, for always being quick and positive, and for keeping me on target through it all. Thanks to Pete Gaughan, senior managing editor, and all around helper with templates. Without these folks and more, this book simply would not have happened.

Thank you,

—Sean

ABOUT THE AUTHOR

Sean **D. Mack, MBA, CISO**, is a visionary and innovative technology leader with a history of driving global business strategy and transformation. He has extensive background in all aspects of technology leadership including DevOps, security, cloud, infrastructure, enterprise applications, development, and program management. Sean is the former CIO and CISO at Wiley, a global research and education company.

Sean has led global teams across a wide range of companies from large financial companies like Experian to innovative tech companies like Etsy. Throughout his career he has held a variety of technology leadership positions ranging from CEO and CTO of a global DevOps consulting firm to Vice President of Operations and Applications for Pearson Education.

Sean has his bachelor's degree in computer and information sciences from the University of California and a master's in business administration from Seattle University.

Sean was born and raised in New York City and has lived in various places around the world including Seattle, Chicago, San Francisco, and the UK. He currently lives in New York with his wife and 9-year-old daughter. He likes fitness, including martial arts and skiing. He rides a Triumph Thruxton and plays upright bass.

How to Contact the Author

Connecting and community are important to DevOps and important to me! If you are passionate about cybersecurity, governance, and technology, I encourage you to connect with me on LinkedIn at www.linkedin.com/in/seandmacknyc. You can also continue the discussion about DevSecOps with me on Twitter at @SeanDMackNYC.

I appreciate your input and questions about this book! If you have feedback or questions, you can contact me on LinkedIn or Twitter, or email me directly at sean@seandmack.com.

INDEX